Researching into Teaching Methods

In Colleges and Universities

**CLINTON BENNETT, LORRAINE FOREMAN-PECK
& CHRIS HIGGINS**

KOGAN
PAGE

The Practical Research Series
Series Editor: Kate Ashcroft

Researching into Assessment and Evaluation in Colleges and Universities,
   Kate Ashcroft and David Palacio
Researching into Teaching Methods in Colleges and Universities,
   Clinton Bennett, Lorraine Foreman-Peck and Chris Higgins

First published in 1996

Kogan Page Limited
120 Pentonville Road
London N1 9JN

© Clinton Bennett, Lorraine Foreman-Peck and Chris Higgins, 1996

British Library Cataloguing in Publication Data

A CIP record for this book is available from the British Library.

ISBN 0 7494 1768 4

Typeset by Kogan Page
Printed and bound in Great Britain by Biddles Ltd, Guildford and King's Lynn

Researching into Teaching Methods

In Colleges and Universities

Contents

List of Research Tasks

Chapter 2

Modified life history method
Collaborative action research
Nominal group technique
Semi-structured interview

Chapter 3

Research diaries: 1
Research diaries: 2
Questionnaire (open)
Evaluation exercise focusing on processes

Chapter 4

Unstructured interview
Self-characterization
Student audit, 5-point scales
Developing an evaluation tool for IT packages
Evaluation exercise focusing on objectives

Chapter 5

Modified focus group technique (photographs)
Modified life history method (snake charts)
Questionnaire (bi-polar)
Participant observation

Chapter 1

Series Introduction

Kate Ashcroft

The research that colleges and universities engage in covers a very wide spectrum, including basic research into fundamental problems as well as entrepreneurial work, often contracted by a particular customer. Each of the books in this series is focused on a particular form of research: that of small-scale insider research. Each looks at issues of teaching, learning and management within colleges and universities. The aim is to provide you with starting points for research that will improve your practice, that of your students and the context for learning and teaching that your institution provides. The research that you undertake may also help you to understand the context in which teaching and learning is managed and should provide you with the raw material for publication in research-based media.

The series is aimed at creating a range of quick and easy to read handbooks, so you can get started on research into aspects of your practice. Each book includes a version of this introductory chapter by the series editor about insider research, its principles and methods. If you have read the series introduction in another of the books in the series, you may wish to skip parts of this chapter and go straight to the section, *Main issues and topics covered in this book* towards the end of this chapter.

Each book in the series also includes a concluding chapter by the series editor that provides guidelines on writing for publication and information about publishing outlets, including an annotated list of publishers and journals interested in educational research in further and higher education in general and teaching methods in particular.

The chapters in this book are focused on contemporary issues. They include a range of examples of research instruments and suggestions as to how you might use or adapt them to your own context for enquiry. The starting points for research cover the following areas:

- the perspectives of the main participants in the educational process;
- the context in which they operate;
- their existing practice;
- their existing values; and
- the relationships between the context and the values and practice.

A range of methods used in insider research in education is included within the research tasks.

The book provides an introduction to some of the issues in teaching and teaching methods in today's competitive climate. It cannot include sufficient information for you to complete a research project for publication. You will need to find out more about the subject matter and the research methodology that you decide to use. Similarly, the books will introduce you to some of the theoretical frameworks open to you, but the discussion will not be deep enough, of itself, to ensure that your research is 'grounded in theory'. For these reasons, an annotated reading list is included at the end of most chapters.

The books in the series should appeal to lecturers in further and higher education who are interested in developing research skills and who would find concrete suggestions for research and some exemplar research questions and instruments helpful. For this reason, the authors have aimed for an accessible and readable style of writing. Care has been taken to keep sentences and paragraphs short and the writing practical, informal and personal. We have tried to avoid using technical terms and jargon unnecessarily, but where these have to be included, we have tried to explain them in as simple a way as possible.

Synopsis of the Series

This book is one of a series that includes the following books:

- *Researching into Assessment and Evaluation in Colleges and Universities* (Ashcroft and Palacio, 1996);
- *Researching into Teaching Methods in Colleges and Universities* (Bennett *et al.*, 1996);
- *Researching into Student Learning and Support in Colleges and Universities* (Ashcroft *et al.*, 1996);
- *Researching into Learning Resources in Colleges and Universities* (Higgins *et al.*, 1996); and

- *Researching into Equal Opportunities in Colleges and Universities* (Ashcroft *et al.*, 1996).

The series aims to provide you with a framework of ideas and starting points for research which can be carried out alongside your current practice. The books present these ideas in such a way that, rather than detracting from your practice, they might enhance it. They introduce methods for you to use (adapted or unadapted) for researching into your own teaching. For example, in Chapter 2, the life history method is described. Most of the ideas do not require visits outside of your institution and suggest data that could be available with a fairly modest outlay of energy.

You should find the books useful if you are new to teaching or if you are an experienced lecturer who needs or wishes to develop a research and publication profile within education. In the case of higher education, this is a major focus that involves all tutors. You may be under pressure to publish for the first time in order to contribute to research rating exercises. You might be undertaking a qualification that includes a research element. A masters degree or doctorate is an increasing requirement for promotion in further and higher education. In the UK, more masters degree courses are being developed and geared towards this sector. In higher education, many staff are now expected to achieve a doctorate. Some of the starting points within this book could be developed into a fairly sophisticated research project.

You may be interested in researching your own practice for its own sake. For instance, you may wish to explore innovative uses of IT to enhance learning. The interest in insider research is percolating into colleges and universities from the action research movement within schools and may grow at a comparable rate.

Insider Research and the Model of Reflection

Insider research is a form of participant research. It is principally about understanding and improving practice within the researcher's institution. It can be focused on a problem and involve cycles of data collection, evaluation and reflection, in which case it is called action research. Carr and Kemmis (1986) provide an easy to read account of the process of action research.

Insider research need not be problem-centred. It is an appropriate approach for a matter of personal curiosity or interest that you decide to investigate in a systematic way. Many tutors who have used the approach have found that insider research is an empowering process. It often comes up with surprises and enables you to see problems in new ways. It is probably the most effective way of exploring the functioning of real-life classrooms and investigating the effects of your interventions. It deals with the real problems and issues you face and, in doing so, may transform those problems and the way you construe teaching and learning. It has a moral base, in that it allows you to explore your actions and those of others in the light of the values that supposedly underpin them.

If you are to be a successful insider researcher, you will need to identify a *critical* group or community that will help you identify appropriate research questions, refine your research instruments and evaluate your reflections and data as you go along. You will also need to seek alternative interpretations of your data from a number of sources and to read widely, in order to locate your insights in a wider context.

When I have engaged in this kind of research and publication, the key thing I have discovered is the need to relate my findings to a theoretical framework (see, for instance, Ashcroft and Griffiths, 1990 or Ashcroft and Peacock, 1993). Very occasionally, I have developed my own framework, but more usually I have used an existing one to analyse my findings. Without such analysis, the results of insider research tend to be anecdotal and descriptive.

The series is built on a theoretical framework provided by the reflective practitioner of education as described by Dewey (1916) and developed by Zeichner, Ashcroft and others (see, for instance, Ashcroft, 1987; Ashcroft and Griffiths, 1989; Deakin, 1982; Isaac and Ashcroft, 1986; Stenhouse, 1979; Zeichner, 1982; Zeichner and Teitlebaum, 1982). The model takes the view that 'knowledge' is not absolute or static and that lecturers in further and higher education should take an active role in constructing and reconstructing it. This process of action does not take place in a social or political vacuum. It is part of the lecturer's role to work collaboratively with others to create morally and educationally justifiable solutions to problems.

This suggests that educationists have some sort of moral responsibility for the truth, and indeed that it is part of their duty to act as whistle-blowers when the powerful define truth in ways convenient for their purposes. It sees reflective practice as much more than a passive 'thinking about'. It embraces active professional development, directed at particular qualities: open-mindedness (a willingness to seek out and take account of the views of a variety of other people), commitment (a real and sustained attachment to the value of your work and to improving its content) and responsibility (a concern with the long- as well as the short-term consequences of action). The enquiry considers the question of 'What works?' but also moves on to pose questions of worthwhileness. This demands investigation into action, intervention and the perspectives of a number of the participants in the educational process: students, tutors, institutional managers, employers, funding agencies and community representatives. It also suggests that intentions, attitudes and values are explored, as well as behaviour and outcomes. Each of the qualities of open-mindedness, commitment and responsibility has particular definitions and demands prerequisite skills and understandings, particularly research skills and skills of analysis. Our intention in introducing you to the research process is to enable you to collect data and to analyse them in the light of your emerging theory of practice (see Argyris and Schon, 1974, for more details of this notion of theory in action.)

I have stated that research skills are an essential prerequisite to reflective practice. This should not be taken to mean that they are sufficient. Reflective practice in teaching also requires that you acquire a range of other skills. These include technical teaching skills, such as voice projection; interpersonal skills such as counselling skills and the ability to work as part of a team; communication skills in a variety of contexts; and the ability to criticize the status quo from a moral point of view. Insider research, perhaps uniquely, can help you to acquire each of these skills. By providing feedback on your actions, insider research directs you to problems that you are creating or failing to solve. You can then experiment with new ways of approaching them and use insider research to provide information on the effectiveness of your new ways of thinking and acting. For instance, in Chapter 2 you are introduced to a method of course evaluation, the nominal group technique.

An elaborated form of this cycle of evaluation, action and data collection is known as action research, and is a particularly potent form of research for developing reflective practice, especially if you test your interpretation of results in a variety of ways: for instance, through using a variety of research methods to look at the same issues or by testing your interpretation of data against those of other parties to the educational process.

Nobody is able to sustain reflective practice at all times. During the process of teaching and research you may frame your problem according to assumptions that you feel comfortable with, you may interpret data to fit your preferred solution or you may fail to notice the most important data. For this reason, we suggest that your methods and interpretation should be made public in some way. You need other people to challenge your assumptions.

Reflective practice requires that you question your deepest beliefs and compare your actions with your values. In doing this, you may find that you must abandon cherished beliefs or practices. Despite the loss that change brings and the risks that it involves, the value of reflective practice is in the process of continual questioning and renewal that is essential for professional development and growth in understanding.

Research Rating

Research can be defined and rated in a variety of ways. For the purposes of this series, I am using the definition of research provided by the Higher Education Funding Council for England (HEFCE, 1994, p.7):

> Research... is... original investigation undertaken in order to gain knowledge and understanding. It includes work of direct relevance to the needs of commerce and industry, as well as to the public and voluntary sectors, scholarship; the invention and generation of ideas, images, performances and artifacts including design, where these lead to new or substantially improved insights; and the use of existing knowledge in experimental development to produce new or substantially improved materials, devices or processes, including design and construction.

Below I describe the system for rating research used in the UK. This is a fairly typical system. Research ratings in other counties will have similarities; some will also have important differences. For instance, the UK research rating exercise does not include any count of the number of times a person's work is cited in others' research.

Most lecturers in higher education are very aware of the imperative to publish and establish a reputation in the world of research and scholarship. In the UK, this imperative has become greater in recent years, with new universities competing in the HEFCE research rating exercise. This exercise affects institutional funding and, if you work in higher education, it is important that you understand the 'rules of the game'. Unfortunately, these are not always explicit and stable. Education at this level is being seen as an increasingly rigorous process. Quality and standards in the sector have come under continuous scrutiny. One of the determinants in the assessment of quality is the level of expertise of staff. Staff who aspire to promotion may have to obtain higher level qualifications that include substantial research (Ashcroft and Foreman-Peck, 1995).

Subject organizational units in higher education are invited to compete for research funding. (Subject organizational units often correspond to subject departments and so, in the interests of readability, I shall refer to them as 'departments' from now on.) The success of departments in generating funded research activity, recruiting research students, employing research staff and enabling individual staff to research and publish determines how much (if any) money is allocated to that institution for research activity. (Of course, if a department is successful, it does not follow that the institution must allocate all the funds it 'wins' to that particular department.) The rating also affects how the department is viewed by the managers of other research funds, potential students and other customers. A high rating may be taken as a rough and ready measure of the quality of research work within a department. It is likely to encourage potential investors to allocate funds to the department and students to apply to it.

The research activity of individual lecturers within a department is therefore an important aspect of the research rating exercise. Interestingly, the research and publication activity of individual lecturers is 'attached' to the individual, rather than the institution where the activity took place. This means that if you are an active researcher, you take your research and publication rating with you when you move job, and so research activity may be the key to your employability.

The operation of research rating exercises can be the subject of investigation in itself. For example, you might explore whether measures that can compare a large number of instances across a sector of education provide opportunities for manipulation by powerful or unscrupulous groups or individuals. Some of these influences might be hard to get at. For instance, the older, more prestigious universities can band together to lobby for measures that favour traditional forms of research or, in countries where the measures include 'citation counts', a group of researchers may operate a 'citation syndicate', each citing the work of the others whenever the opportunity arises.

Starting Points for Research: Values and Practice

We do not provide a total blueprint for research. This would be impossible, given the variety of contexts in which the readers of the series work and the variety of findings they are likely to come up with. Even if it were possible to lay out a complete research project for you to follow, we would not wish to do so. A large part of the new knowledge and understanding gained from research comes from the stimulus to creativity that asking your own questions and looking at preliminary data provide. In collecting your own data, and then asking questions of yourself such as, 'What do I need to know to interpret these data?', 'How can I get at the meanings behind these data?' or, 'What other data do I need?', you will come up with transformational resolutions to research questions that are far more innovative and creative than any the authors could suggest. Therefore, you should feel free to interpret research tasks widely: to adapt and alter suggested foci for research and ideas for data collection to fit your own context and, most importantly, to go beyond the first cycle of data collection to ask your own questions.

It is important to be aware of the limitations of small-scale research. If you claim a spurious objectivity to your work, you are likely to miss the most important strength of insider research: the opportunity it offers to you to explore your existing practice and that of others, the stated values that underpin this practice and the relationship between those values and the practice. Practice may seem to you to be the most objective of these elements but, in exploring practice, it is important to realize that it is often more difficult to get at it than first appears. There is often a gap between what people (including you) say and believe that they do and what they actually do. Thus, self-report may not capture the data you need. Other methods are mediated by the values of the person undertaking the analysis. For instance, if you want to assess the effectiveness of using IT to carry out assessment, the results you get may depend upon the categories you choose to organize the data.

Each of us has values that we espouse. Many teachers can articulate them in relation to certain criteria. For example, most of us believe in equal opportunity. You may want to dig deeper than this to explore how equal opportunities are defined by teachers and how these definitions are or may be incompatible. The series explores the values that are held by each of the stakeholders in education, the implications of these for teaching, learning and management, and the extent to which they are compatible or raise dilemmas that must be resolved. For example, student diversity is discussed in Chapter 2 and institutional ethos is discussed in Chapter 5.

Perspectives to be Researched

Reflective practice is about taking account of the viewpoints of others and the long as well as the short term consequences of your action. For this reason, the series covers the investigation of a variety of perspectives, including:

- students;
- lecturers;
- providers of educational support services;
- institutional managers;
- employers;
- funding agencies; and
- the local community.

Each of these groups has its own priorities and the people working within them have their own satisfactions and frustrations. The quality of the services that an institution provides in support of student learning is in part determined by these perspectives.

Among the research issues covered in the books are:

- the link between values and practice;
- the perceptions and attitudes of each of the stakeholders in education;
- the link between attitudes and behaviour;
- educational and non-educational priorities of each of the stakeholders in education;
- issues of efficiency and effectiveness;
- definitions of the problems education faces;
- criteria by which success or failure in dealing with these problems may be judged;
- objectives, processes or outcomes;
- relationships between people;
- issues of justice, equality and the ways that diversity is catered for within education;
- conflicting interests with education;
- ethics and the exploration of dilemmas; and
- control issues in learning.

These issues are described in more detail in the introductory chapter to Ashcroft and Palacio (1996).

Research in education may fall into the quantitative tradition and focus on the collection (usually of large numbers) of numerical data, or into the qualitative tradition and look in depth at a smaller number of instances. It may be focused on 'discovery' or on the improvement of practice. Much ideological baggage now surrounds the qualitative and quantitative traditions in education. You need to get to grips with this debate in order that you understand the strengths and weaknesses of each. Within education there has been a shift from respect for models of research based on the scientific tradition of experimental and quasi-experimental research methods towards qualitative, descriptive methods within naturalistic settings, first pioneered in subjects such as anthropology and now termed 'ethnographic' methods. Each of these models has its strength and weakness. The qualitative tradition is criticized because of its limited scope, particularity and 'subjectivity', the quantitative tradition because of the triviality of its findings, their lack of application to the real life 'messiness' of classrooms and because most practitioners of such research were expert in research and not in education, and therefore addressed other researchers, rather than teachers. More details about the controversies that surround each of these traditions and the limitations and opportunities presented by each may be found in the introductory chapter to Ashcroft and Palacio (1996).

Data Collection Techniques

The authors provide you with starting points only for research. These cover a very wide range of research methods. It is impossible to provide a comprehensive list of issues related to each of those methods within a book of this length. The best we can do is to present to you the major strengths and weaknesses of each, and to refer you to other sources where you can read more about the technical issues involved in using the research tools you have chosen (See the annotated reading list at the end of this chapter.)

Most of the research suggested in the series is small-scale and local and so we do not discuss methods of statistical analysis. It may be that you become inspired to undertake a more major study, in which case there are a variety of computer programs that may help you to analyse your data (see Chapter 4 and the Appendix), or you may find a book such as Cohen and Manion (1985) useful. If you intend to use statistical analysis, it is important that you make this decision at the start of the data collection process. The method you use will affect the form of the data you should collect. You will probably find all sorts of problems if you collect your data and then look round for a means of analysing it.

Questionnaires provide a means of obtaining information about people's attitudes, thoughts and feelings in a relatively time-efficient way. They cannot tell you much about actual behaviour since what people say and what they do are not always the same. Questionnaires may be more or less structured. The advantage of structured questionnaires is that, in closing the response options that you allow, you make it possible to handle more data and to compare one set of data with another. On the other hand, unstructured or semi-structured questionnaires allow the respondents to express more exactly what they wish to say. In this sense they are a more accurate reflection of reality. Unfortunately, the very richness of the data makes them difficult to handle. It requires you to impose some sort of order, so that you can communicate trends and issues to your audience. This may oversimplify the responses in the same way as a more structured questionnaire.

The data that questionnaires yield are only as good as the returns you get and questions you use. You will usually get a better return if you can hand the questionnaires to a group to fill in in your presence. The construction of a questionnaire is a skilled matter. For instance, you will need to ensure that your questions are not ambiguous, that they get at what you think they do and that they are expressed simply and in a non-threatening way. (See Ashcroft, Bigger and Coates, 1996, for details of how to construct a questionnaire.)

Standardized tests are commonly in the form of questionnaires. They are useful for getting at issues such as learning or management style and attitudes and beliefs. Like questionnaires or interviews, they are not good at describing behaviour. For example, so-called aptitude tests do not describe what you will actually do in a given situation, but merely predict how well you will perform according to the similarity of your responses to those of people doing that job, or your ability as gauged by fairly crude measures in areas such as problem solving, literacy and numeracy. Standardized tests have the advantage that they have been validated professionally and so enable you to compare your findings with those obtained in other times and places, but you may need to clear copyright to use them.

Interviews share the problems and advantages of the questionnaire, except that they are much more time-consuming to carry out, but yield richer data. There may be more of a tendency for the respondents to say what they think you wish to hear. This may be a particular problem in insider research, where the respondents may have a personal relationship with you and where issues of power (yours over them, or theirs over you) may intrude and make truly honest responses difficult.

One form of interview that enables you to get open responses from a number of people without the problem of obtaining data that are too unmanageable is the group interview. In the form of focus groups, this technique has been used effectively within market research and is beginning to be applied in education (Davies and Headington, 1995). The group interview enables a number of respondents to express themselves in their own way and for you to check out with the respondents your interpretation of what they are saying and the ways you might categorize their responses. You thereby avoid some of the problems of other unstructured techniques. However, some respondents may influence the others' responses unduly and some may be disempowered or find it hard to express themselves in a group situation. Group interviewing is thus a skilled business.

Observation is probably the only way of getting at behaviour, but it may not tell you about motivation, thoughts feelings and attitudes. Observation may be unstructured: for example, fly-on-the-wall descriptions of what is happening in a situation. A structured observation schedule may enable you to count the frequency of particular pieces of behaviour. If you use structured observation, you are likely to find your data fairly easy to handle, but you may find that categorizing behaviour is not at all straightforward in practice. If this is not recognized in the way you present your findings, you may make your conclusions appear more clear cut than they are. On the other hand, you will probably have to impose order on your fly-on-the-wall observations. Again you will probably have to simplify reality in order to do so.

Scenario analysis is one way of eliciting people's deeper thoughts and feeling. Scenarios can be presented to respondents in the form of pictures, stories or using some other medium. You might then ask them to explore various aspects of their response. You could record these responses using any one of a variety of structured and unstructured instruments: for example, a snake chart is described in Chapter 5.

Scenarios tend to be contrived to enable you to get at whatever issue you are interested in. Another form of data collection that requires less direct intervention, and so is perhaps less disturbing to the data, is biographical writing (see for instance, Connolly and Clandinin, 1990; Cortazzi, 1993). In biographical or narrative analysis, you ask respondents to describe significant events, with more or less guidance from you as to the aspects that they should focus upon. For example, if you were interested in the factors that enable women to succeed with their studies, you might ask several successful women to produce a 'story', not necessarily in words: you can use other techniques such as asking respondents to depict their life as a journey, road or a 'temperature' chart, showing the peaks and troughs in their lives, related to particular events. The data can then be analysed for particular patterns of influence. As with all forms of stimulated recall, you need to be aware that what people tell you, and what they believe about their history, especially their more significant or more remote history, may be clouded by a number of factors. While biography can tell you about people's perceptions, it does not necessarily tell you about what actually happened nor what was cause and what was effect.

Diaries and field notes allow you to collect a range of information as it occurs, using question and answer techniques with individuals or groups, observations and so on, in order to analyse and interpret it at a later date (see for instance, Burgess, 1984 for suggestions as to how to go about this). You can also ask others to keep diaries for you in order to capture their experience more immediately. This techniques allows you to explore phenomena in as natural a setting as possible. On the other hand, it does rely on you (or your subjects) noticing and recording significant events, generally in the course of a busy day. This can be difficult.

From the discussion of data collection methods above, it is clear that structured techniques require you to determine categories of response before you start. In order to do so with any confidence, you may have to undertake a pilot study of some kind or to test your hunches about categories in some way. More unstructured techniques require you to explore the data once they are collected to find what categories emerge.

There is a wealth of interesting evidence to be gleaned from systems analysis and the interrogation of databases within your institution. The systems within your institution will contain data that relate to student admissions, locations, subjects and their progress; library and other purchases and stock; personnel; various sorts of accounts, institutional statistics that relate to the physical and learning environment; and performance indicators that may be used for a variety of purposes. Alternatively, you might explore the way that systems are experienced by one or other of the parties to education or the way people and items are categorized.

Documents are part of the public face of institutional activity. Examining the hidden messages within them can be useful and interesting. Documents affect relationships within the institution at all levels. They influence operations and strategy within the institution and are of interest if you want to explore the match between the aspirations of the various parties to education and institutional policies. It can be interesting to analyse what people say, what they do and the way that they present themselves. For example, you might look at the ways that members of certain groups are reflected in official documents, or the ways that expressed aims are or are not reflected in other documents.

13

You might wish to create other records that can be explored in some depth. For example, you might video, tape record or photograph certain situations in order to analyse what was going on. A research task using photography is suggested in Chapter 5.

Case studies provide a means of bringing a range of techniques to bear in order to describe what is going on in a particular situation or with a particular group of people. As such, they are especially useful within the kind of insider research that is trying to get at a complex issue. They enable the researcher to use a variety of data collection techniques to look at a variety of viewpoints. Somebody, generally the person who has collected them, has to interpret the data. For this reason, a case study cannot be 'objective' nor does it automatically ascribe cause and effect without bias. Interpretations should, where possible, be checked with respondents to maximize the validity of the findings (see Chapter 5).

The important thing is never to claim more for your research than is justified by your methods, the data you have collected and your analysis. Insider research can sometimes empower the reader, who may be inspired by a report of research into practice that chimes with their own experience. It is almost impossible to prove anything in education. You need to be very tentative in your conclusions. Because it is almost impossible to isolate variables in real educational situations, it is seldom possible to say that a particular stimulus *caused* a particular *effect*. Even if you get apparently clear-cut results, generally the best that can be said is that, in the circumstances you investigated, it appears that one thing may be *associated* with another.

Main Issues and Topics Covered in this Book

Chapter 2 – current issues facing lecturers, namely teaching larger numbers, increased diversity of students' experience and formal academic attainment, and changing perceptions of the lecturer's role within the teaching-learning process.

Chapter 3 – use of collaborative and resource-based teaching-learning methods as possible responses to the challenges identified in Chapter 2.

Chapter 4 – how changing perceptions of lecturers' roles and demand for the vocationalization of the curriculum affects lecturers' sense of professional identity and their understanding of the disciplines or subjects they teach, using resource-based learning and IT as examples.

Chapter 5 – institutional and interpersonal factors in initiating change in teaching methods and how lecturers can operate as effective agents of change within these contexts.
Appendix – use of IT for analysis of qualitative research.

Annotated Reading List

Argyris, C and Schon, D (1974) *Theory into Practice*, Beckenham: Croom Helm.
   The definitive book on the relationships between the theories that people hold about their teaching and the theories that they develop in action.
Ashworth, A and Harvey, R (1993) *Quality in Further and Higher Education*, London: Jessica Kingsley.
   An account of Total Quality Management, performance indicators, and systems for assessing standards.
Brown, S, Jones, G and Rawnsley, S (eds) (1993) *Observing Teaching*, Birmingham: Staff and Educational Development Association.
   This focuses on inquiring into practice in colleges and universities. It covers issues in the appraisal of teaching (who should do it, what should be observed and how). The focus is on professional development, rather than research within higher education.
Bell, J (1993) *Doing your Research Project*, 2nd edn, Milton Keynes: Open University Press.
   This book deals with research across the disciplines, rather than teaching and learning in further and higher education.
Cohen, L and Manion, L (1985) *Research Methods in Education*, 2nd edn, Beckenham: Croom Helm.
   A comprehensive account of the major research methods in education. It is not easy to read, and I would argue with its assumption that educational research should be scientific, but its critique of the approach we adopt provides a useful counterbalance. The book covers most of the techniques in educational research, as well as more technical aspects such as grid analysis and multidimensional measurement.
Gibbs, G *et al.* (1988) *53 Interesting Things to do...*, Bristol: TES.
   This series is very popular and sells well (one book is in its fourth edition since 1986). These are about 140–160 pages long and provided some useful starting points for thinking about teaching and learning. The focus is on practice, rather than research, but this can provide you with a basis for an evaluation or intervention study.
Green, D (1993) *What is Quality in Higher Education?*, Buckingham: Open University Press.
   A report of a national research project on the assessment of quality in higher education.

Hammersley, M and Atkinson, P (1983) *Ethnography Principles in Practice*, London: Tavistock Publications.
A reasonably accessible account of ethnographic methods and their relationship to the social world. It includes a critical analysis of case study, observation, interviewing and ways of filing and recording data.

McKernan, J (1991) *Curriculum Action Research: A handbook of methods and resources for the reflective practitioner*, London: Kogan Page.
This book is a good introduction to action research. It contains many useful suggestions for collecting data.

Smith, B and Brown, S (eds) (1994) *Research, Teaching and Learning in Higher Education*, London: Kogan Page.
A collection of reports of research undertaken by experienced education developers within higher education.

References

Argyris, C and Schon, D (1974) *Theory into Practice*, Beckenham: Croom Helm.

Ashcroft, K, (1987) 'The history of an innovation', *Assessment and Evaluation in Higher Education*, 12, 1, 37–45.

Ashcroft, K. and Foreman-Peck, L. (1995) *The Lecturer's Guide to Quality and Standards in Colleges and Universities*, London: Falmer Press.

Ashcroft, K and Griffiths, M (1989) 'Reflective teachers and reflective tutors: School experience in and initial teacher education course', *Journal of Education for Teaching*, 15, 1, 35–52.

Ashcroft, K and Griffiths, M (1990) 'Action research in initial teacher education', in Zuber-Skerritt, O (ed.) *Action Research in Higher Education*, Brisbane: Griffith University Press.

Ashcroft, K and Palacio, D (1996) *Researching into Assessment and Evaluation in Colleges and Universities*, London: Kogan Page.

Ashcroft, K and Peacock, E (1993) 'An evaluation of the progress, experience and employability of mature students on the BEd course at Westminster College, Oxford', *Assessment and Evaluation in Higher Education*, 18, 1, 57–70.

Ashcroft, K, Bigger, S and Coates, D (1996) *Researching into Equal Opportunities in Colleges and Universities*, London: Kogan Page.

Ashcroft, K, Jones, M and Siraj-Blatchford, J (1996) *Researching into Student Learning and Support in Colleges and Universities*, London: Kogan Page.

Bennett, C, Foreman-Peck, F and Higgins, C (1996) *Researching into Teaching Methods in Colleges and Universities*, London: Kogan Page.

Burgess, R (1984) 'Keeping a research diary', in Bell, J and Goulding, S (eds) *Conducting Small Scale Investigations in Education Management*, London: Harper and Row.

Carr, W and Kemmis, S (1986) *Becoming Critical: Knowing through action research*, London: Falmer Press.

Cohen, L and Manion, L (1985) *Research Methods in Education*, 2nd edn, Beckenham: Croom Helm.

Connolly, FM and Clandinin, DJ (1990) 'Stories of experience and narrative enquiry', *Educational Researcher*, 19, 5, 2–14.

Cortazzi, M (1993) *Narrative Analysis*, London: Falmer Press.

Davies, S and Headington, R (1995) 'The focus group as an educational research method', *British Educational Research Association Annual Conference*, Oxford: October.

Deakin University (1982) *The Action Research Reader*, Victoria: Deakin University Press.

Dewy, J (1916) *Democracy and Education*, New York: The Free Press.

Elliott, J (1991) *Action Research for Educational Change*, Buckingham: Open University Press.

Higgins, C, Reading, J and Taylor, P (1996) *Researching into Learning Resources in Colleges and Universities*, London: Kogan Page.

Higher Education Funding Council for England (1994) *Research Assessment Exercise*, June. Bristol: HEFCE.

Isaac, J and Ashcroft, K (1986) 'A leap into the practical', in Nias, J and Groundwater-Smith, S (eds) *The Enquiring Teacher: Supporting and sustaining teacher research*, London: Falmer Press.

Stenhouse, L (1979) 'What is action research?', *CARE*, University of East Anglia, Norwich, mimeograph.

Zeichner, K (1982) 'Reflective teaching and field-based experience in teacher education', *Interchange*, 12, 4, 1–22.

Zeichner, K and Teitlebaum, K (1982) 'Personalised and inquiry oriented education: An analysis of two approaches to the development of curriculum in field-based experience', *Journal of Education for Teaching*, 8, 2, 95–117.

Chapter 2

Contemporary Directions for Research into Teaching

Introduction

In this chapter we aim to look at current challenges facing lecturers in colleges and universities and to draw on research where appropriate. We have concentrated on the changing professional identity of the lecturer, the challenge presented by wider student diversity (in experience and formal academic attainments), and the problem of increased group sizes. We will highlight those areas which need further research work. The use of information technology in researching and solving teaching problems is discussed in Chapter 4 and the Appendix.

Policy initiatives in higher and further education, such as the introduction of National Vocational Qualifications (NVQs) and widened access, have demanded, and are likely to continue to demand, a radical reappraisal of the lecturer's role. Lecturers will increasingly be expected to have well-informed views on professional issues. In a situation of increased class size for example, questions about the quality of provision have to be asked. This raises further questions, ethical and practical, about the way in which lecturers should be involved with research into teaching and learning and the sort of answers practitioner research can give. It is a presumption of this chapter that small-scale practitioner research can enhance your professional development and that such experience, if presented in a systematic way, is of interest to other practitioners. The kind of research advocated here is directed to increasing your insight and understanding, in a morally acceptable way.

Background

The late 1980s saw a rapid change to a mass higher education system coupled with reduced resources. This has led to the recognition that colleges and universities must become learning organizations if the quality of teaching and learning is not to decline (Elton, 1994). There is growing concern that some assessment innovations are being introduced in order to save lecturers' time rather than for sound pedagogical principles (McDowell and Mowl, 1995). Teaching quality assessments, carried out by HEFCE and OFSTED, are placing greater emphasis on the professional aspects of the lecturer's role. The drive for more efficient modes of delivery is leading to unforeseen consequences that, it is argued, threaten the quality of learning. An example of a recent innovation in Britain is the adoption of semesters instead of terms as the unit of course delivery. There are claims that this is leading to an impossible assessment burden and that shortened courses are not suitable for in-depth study (*THES*, 1995).

It has been suggested that current circumstances demand a move away from the idea of a lecturer who simply delivers a course to the idea of the lecturer who researches the delivery of courses as part of the teaching and learning process (Elton, 1994). The concept of practitioner research, as a method of professional development, is well established at the primary and secondary phases of education. (Practitioner research or insider research is described more fully in Chapter 1.)

An alternative way of thinking about the role of research is in terms of 'pure' and 'applied'. There is a body of research findings undertaken by full-time researchers into higher education which has provided a conceptual framework for describing and researching teaching problems. Their findings have been presented as universal truths, ie, as holding for all students in all contexts. One such claim will serve as an illustration:

> Students tend to take a surface approach (*to learning*) when the
> workload is perceived to be heavy, where the assessment system is
> perceived to demand, reward or tolerate memorisation and in a
> number of other known circumstances (Gibbs, preface, 1994,
> emphasis added).

Practitioner research can usefully draw on findings such as these, testing such claims against your own experience.

It is our view, however, that the most appropriate model for lecturers is the practitioner research model since it starts with the immediate 'felt concerns' of the individual and is owned by the individual. Practitioner research is grounded in personal experience and informed by research literature. This does not necessarily mean that the wheel has to be reinvented each time an issue such as self-assessment is addressed. Lessons can be learnt from the accumulating insights of others and basic research into the psychology of learning.

The movement towards a learning organization may be compromised by the self-image of the lecturer as an expert solely in a discipline rather than as an expert additionally in others learning. This is a real dilemma since lecturers are hired, rightly so, for their subject expertise. Institutional structures have supported this view and the present research assessment exercise has reinforced this view. Expertise in pedagogical matters may be seen as an unwelcome diversion of energy. This conflict of interest is explored in Chapter 4.

Another impediment to the development of research activity has been the idea that excellence in teaching is a nebulous one incapable of specification (eg, Loder *et al.*, 1989). However, if one argues that excellence in teaching should have as its measure the quality of student learning, rather than personal qualities such as enthusiasm, then it may be possible to develop criteria which will allow one to judge which learning regimes are more conducive to learning than others. Enthusiasm is important, but other factors may be more important, such as a student's approach to study. There is a body of research which is informative here (see, for example, Ramsden, 1992).

Increased 'consumer' awareness on the part of government, students and parents, does however require a reformulation of lecturers' identity to accommodate a more sophisticated understanding of the processes of teaching and learning.

The Changing Professional Identity of the Lecturer, Teaching Methods and Course Design

We have started the research with the problem of professional identity, since it is fundamental to teaching. There are several dimensions to the need to be aware of your own values and possibly unexamined assumptions in your role as an educator. This can be seen if you consider situations where you may be expected to teach in a way that you consider wholly inappropriate for your discipline, for example teaching literature to groups of 400. If your idea of the value of literature as a worthwhile enterprise is fundamentally tied to the idea of helping students develop their own responses rather than taking over the responses of others, then it is hard to see what can be meaningfully achieved in such a setting. Indeed this aim would be difficult to realize in groups above 20.

Good teaching is dependent on commitment to views about what learning a particular subject/discipline fundamentally consists of. Education generally can be regarded as an induction into the standards and ways of thinking that belong to disciplines. This is true even where there are radical differences in the ways that a discipline can be construed, as in English literature. One aspect of professional identity is knowing very clearly what you are trying to achieve. What for example do you expect your best students to have achieved? What intellectual skills should they have developed? What counts as progress and development in your subject or discipline? What sort of values do you want your students to be committed to? The answers to these questions have implications for your views about teaching methods, group size and course design.

There is a growing body of research into the element of reflexivity in the professional development of secondary and primary teachers, using life history methods (for example, Landgrebe and Winter, 1994; Sikes *et al.*, 1985; Thomas, 1995). Being aware of your own values is particularly important in that version of practitioner research called 'practical deliberative action research' (Carr and Kemmis, 1986). One way of guarding against interpreting data in accordance with your own preferred viewpoint is to become aware of your own beliefs and values. The life history method usually involves in-depth interviews with a researcher who seeks to elicit your life story by examining key turning points. This method has been used to study the professional identity of secondary school teachers at a time of crisis (Sikes *et al.*, 1985). One of us has adapted the method to enable lecturers to write about their life histories as part of a professional development course. In order to protect lecturers who may see this kind of research as potentially intrusive and possible damaging we have asked them to share only with her those aspects of their experience they would like her to read about. Confidentiality has to be assured unless permission to use the material is given by the author. In the research task below you are invited to write freely under whichever headings seem most appropriate. This exercise should help you clarify your views.

RESEARCH TASK. MODIFIED LIFE HISTORY METHOD

You are invited to write about your life history. As a starting point for writing, choose whichever question seems most appropriate:

- Why did you choose to teach?
- What part of your work gives you most satisfaction? Why? Has this changed over time?
- Have you ever faced a crisis a work? How did you resolve it?

- Was any particular person influential in the your development as a lecturer? In what way?
- Do you regret any decisions you made in the past? Why?
- Has any piece of legislation had an effect on your career?
- What is the hardest aspect of your work at the moment? What makes it difficult?

A further dimension in the development of a professional identity is strong departmental expectations concerning good teaching. In the current research literature on teaching and learning in higher education, these aspects of a lecturer's professional identity are unacknowledged. There is an unexamined assumption that lecturers are autonomous and able to teach what they like, as they like. Certainly this was a claim made in the White Paper, *The Development of Higher Education into the 1990s* (DES, 1985) where it was argued that higher education was failing in its duty to prepare students for wealth creation since lecturers were following their own interests.

There is some research to show (and much anecdotal evidence) that where a lecturer departs radically from the custom and practice of the department there are seriously unpleasant consequences (Schwartz and Webb, 1993). Many courses are delivered by a team of lecturers either sequentially or with parallel classes. Here the lecturer may have to come to terms with the course team's values and methods, which may be coherent and explicitly published (see, for example, Foreman-Peck *et al.*, 1992) or the values and beliefs within the team may be contentious and disputed. Before any attempt to research into your own practice, you should be able to answer the following questions: What are the principal methods of teaching used in your department and on courses you contribute to? What kind of learning outcome do they seem to encourage?

Research into teaching and learning should, in an ethical and a prudent sense, be conducted within the parameters of a departmental view about what learning a discipline consists of and should be actively supported by departments. It is unlikely that new professional identities, built on research into pedagogy, will flourish in an indifferent environment. In the primary and secondary sectors of education the ideal model of bringing about improvement in problematic circumstances is collaborative action research. Summarizing his learning from 30 years involvement in teaching and working with teachers on school based action research projects, Elliot (1993, p.176) says that, individual teachers cannot significantly improve their practices in isolation without opportunities for discussion with professional peers and others operating in a significant role relationship with them.

It is our view that this is true for most of us working in higher and further education today. The need for greater efficiency may prompt course teams to take part in decisions about changes in course delivery.

The central issue has become the nature of the relationship between management structures and personal agency in shaping pedagogical practices. The present situation can be characterized as one of imposed change, a matter of top-down reorganization. In higher education this has meant increased class sizes, shared teaching (ie, where two different courses join for some or most teaching sessions) and/or the move to resource-based flexible learning, and open and distance learning courses. Evaluation is generally by indicators of effective organizational functioning. For example high student drop-out rates might be an indicator of ineffective course delivery. The key question for managers is, 'Can quality be maintained while increasing numbers of students and reducing cost?'

However, innovations can only be made to work by lecturers evaluating processes according to agreed ideas about quality in learning. Unless there is a dialogue between lecturers and managers there will inevitably be a dilution of quality. Research directed at values clarification is an important step in specifying success criteria which are internal to the learning process. The specification of such criteria enables the internal monitoring of course and student progression. Pedagogical values clarification includes the values of all partners in the learning process. Thus student satisfaction and insights into the processes of teaching and learning are important. These values may be very basic ones involving, for example, student safety. Imagine the dilemma for the horticultural lecturer who has been used to doing practical work with small groups, because of the dangers of accidents with spades, in finding that he now has a group of over 100 students!

Collaborative action research is a method of practitioner research focused on such pedagogical problems as that given in the example above and involves lecturers in the process of specifying the problem, trying a solution, monitoring its implementation, and evaluating its success. Evaluation derives its standards from teachers' educational values or success criteria. From a managerial perspective such an enterprise may seem irrelevant or at best marginal. However, if innovations are to be implemented without loss of quality such effort on the part of lecturers is crucial. We explore innovation and change in Chapter 5.

The version of action research called 'critical action research' sets out to solve practical problems but locates them within a Marxist perspective (Carr and Kemmis, 1986). The idea is that practitioners can emancipate their teaching from systems which are oppressive. This involves practitioners in defining the structural properties which shape their practices. Once enlightened, lecturers are in a position to engage in 'political' action to reconstruct institutional practices. An example of this kind of emancipatory research has been carried out in the nursing profession by Titchin and Binnie (1993).

An example of an institutional practice in higher education is semesterization – a fairly recent innovation in Britain, although it is well established in the USA. This practice could be said to embody the principle of increased student choice enabling students to take courses that most closely fit their particular interests. Semesterization has, however, created problems for lecturers and students. Unless lecturers and students change their practices, semesterization will fail and the principle it embodies will not be realized.

That changes are being implemented without these issues being addressed is evident from the letter pages of the *Times Higher Educational Supplement*. One correspondent poses the question, 'Why is this madness called semesterization happening?' She claims that in many institutions the new modular semesterized year has left students 'confused and anxious', staff 'running in ever decreasing circles trying to meet unreasonable deadlines' so that formal assessments can take place twice a year instead of once (*THES*, 24 February 1995). Students are complaining as well. In the same issue of the *THES*, Richards reports that students at Liverpool John Moores University are to be balloted by their union over the timing of semester-end examinations. Students are confronted by assessment overload, lecturers feel under pressure to cram in content.

Enough is known now about the introduction of innovations to predict that hierarchically imposed ones will tend to be resisted or resented (Fullan and Hargreaves, 1992).

Problems of increased assessment loads due to increased student numbers and semesterization can provide the motivation for thinking and research. An important starting point is sharing with colleagues personal educational values. For example it may be that semesterization provides a choice between depth and breadth, and that for some students breadth is appropriate. It may be that choices of modules can be directed according to this principle. The point and purposes of assessment should be shared and agreed. It may be that forms of assessments can be found which do not have to be 'traditional' once their purpose is agreed. Collaborative action research methodology provides a systematic way of tackling these issues. It involves group discussion and identification of problems, values clarification, and systematic evaluation of data. In this context, pure research can be helpful. For example, it is now well established from research findings that a very heavy burden of assessment leads to students adopting dysfunctional learning strategies. Findings from research can inform the conversation that lecturers' teams should be having, but they are no substitute for practitioner research.

There are a number of reports which document the implementation of innovations carried out according to action research methodology. These accounts of the story of innovations provide insights for other practitioners in the same field. A good example is given in Pendry's (1990) account of the trials and tribulations of setting up an internship scheme for student teachers. This study would be of interest to anyone challenged with setting up new forms of work-based learning.

The following research task outlines the practical-deliberative action research framework, taking your idea for practitioner research and following it through. This framework is described in diagrammatic form in Ashcroft and Palacio (1996, ch.6).

RESEARCH TASK. COLLABORATIVE ACTION RESEARCH

Research Focus

1. Is any aspect of your course or institutional arrangements not working, eg, semesterization, mass lectures, seminar groups, resource-based learning, the role of computers in learning, work placements, syndicate groups, peer assessments, quality of student learning, open and distance learning? (An easy to read description of these teaching methods can be found in Ashcroft and Foreman-Peck, 1994.)

If so, try keeping a research diary, noting substantive events (for example, when, where and with whom things happen) and what you find out about your own beliefs and values. Try to get clear the grounds of your feeling that things aren't right. After a suitable period of reflection try to formulate some research questions, to further explore the issues. Try to interest other staff in the issue, especially your manager. If your institution has an educational development unit you may be able to attract some research assistance. Collaboration is essential to the success and credibility of your research project. It is also important that your research is ethically uncontentious. You should consult your institution's ethical code concerning research activity.

---

2. Collect information from staff and students to determine whether the problem is more general. There are many data collection methods for doing this (see Chapter 1). A questionnaire to students may be more appropriate if large numbers are involved. Group discussion may be more appropriate where you have easy access to the people involved and the numbers are small. It may be appropriate to ask students to keep logs for short periods. You may wish to consider some of the data analysis techniques described in the Appendix, if they are appropriate to your particular context.

Plan an Intervention

3. With other staff (and if appropriate, students) involved in the research, try to formulate a solution to the problem. Ask the following questions:

What is happening now?
Why is it problematic?
What can be done about it?
What would count as an improvement?
What pedagogic principles are conserved or lost in a proposed change?

Implement and Monitor

4. Implement and monitor your solution. You will need to collect and analyse data in order to decide whether the innovation has brought about improvement.

Evaluate

5. If the innovation has been successful you may wish to write it up. Good guidelines for writing up this kind of research are given by Elliott (1991). Basically, it takes a narrative form, so it is essential that some kind of research diary is kept. If the research has not been successful, you may wish to reconsider and modify the innovatory step and try again.

Student Diversity

With the introduction of the assessment of prior learning (APL) and the assessment of prior experiential learning (APEL), old assumptions about the student body are no longer valid. Much traditional teaching in higher education depended on the assumption that groups were homogeneous in terms of age, academic achievements and aspirations. In the case of student aspirations or orientations to their study it has been found, on the contrary, that there are quite considerable differences between students. Taylor (1978) carried out a longitudinal qualitative study on student orientations. She identified four distinct types of orientation: the academic, the vocational, the personal and the social. These categories were further elaborated, so that for example in the personal category a student's overriding concern might be with challenging material, whereas another's might be with proof of capability. The first orientation is aimed at self-improvement, the second at compensation or feedback.

The concept of orientation is useful in that it can serve to help lecturers understand different reactions or behaviour of students to the same course. It can also explain why we may feel more sympathetic to some students rather than others. Practitioner research into student orientation could inform course design since it prompts questions about course aims. For example, we could ask ourselves to what extent our courses provide feedback and reassurance for those needing proof of capability, or how far they allow for extended and optional challenges. For those students with vocational orientations, is there a clear idea of relevance of course aims to vocational outcomes?

In a study of women returners to higher education, Mezirow (1981) found that most had experienced a 'disorienting dilemma'. In interviews, the students reported that they had undergone a 'perspective transformation' which had led to a questioning of their gender roles. Willy Russell's play, 'Educating Rita', explores the same phenomenon. It has been noted that on certain professional development courses, failure can have consequences for career development and professional reputation. These courses, such as the MEd at Westminster College Oxford, can generate a high degree of anxiety which is not conducive to a good learning climate. We have already referred to the finding by Ramsden (1992) and others that a very heavy assessment burden leads to students adopting coping strategies to get by, and that the possibility of meaningful learning is sacrificed. Thus the way in which students experience a course as well as the orientation they bring to it are vitally important in informing the kind of teaching strategy to be adopted. For example, at Westminster, students are given opportunities to negotiate the curriculum (within a framework), they are invited to evaluate the course at a mid-term point, and individual students are granted permission to 'grab the floor' for five minutes to share any problems they may be experiencing.

If you are interested in this area you might start by carrying out a course evaluation designed to elicit student experiences. An excellent technique is the nominal group technique (NGT) which tends to elicit responses ranging from satisfaction or dissatisfaction with room temperature to assessment burdens (Gibbs *et al.*, 1988, pp.77–9). The results of such an evaluation can be used as further material for discussion.

RESEARCH TASK. NOMINAL GROUP TECHNIQUE

1. With a course in mind ask students to consider two questions:

    Which aspects of the course have helped my learning?
    Which aspects of the course have hindered my learning?

2. Students should spend a few minutes individually brainstorming answers to these questions. Each student's complete list of helpful and unhelpful items is read out. The lecturer records them on a flipchart. Duplicated items are crossed out and ambiguous items are discussed with the tutor so that the intended meaning is clear to all.
3. Each item is numbered.
4. Students are asked to rank them in order of importance.
5. The lecturer analyses the results.

The ground rules for the NGT are important. To prevent group intimidation, no student should speak, apart from the student being addressed by the lecturer. The lecturer should not evaluate the items being offered, but should clarify and record. This is important if you are to find out what is really bothering or interesting a group. No student or tutor should be named, since the evaluation is concerned with issues not personalities. Further discussion of this technique is to be found in Ashcroft and Foreman-Peck (1994).

Relatively new aspects of teaching such as peer assessment, syndicate working or resource-based learning lack well-documented case studies and are worth exploring.

Research into student learning found that successful learners used different strategies and had a different conception of learning, compared to less successful learners (Marton and Saljo, 1984). The two approaches are called deep learning (the successful approach) and surface learning (the less successful approach) (see Chapter 4 for a more detailed discussion of these approaches). Other researchers found that assessment overload or course content overload tended to promote a surface approach to learning (Ramsden, 1992). Recognizing the influence which assessment has on student learning, there has been an interest in developing forms of assessment which are more conducive to a deep approach to learning. As McDowell and Mowl (1995) point out, research in the area has been concerned with the reliability of innovative assessments, for example peer assessment, and there has been little research into students' perceptions of the impact of new assessment methods on their learning.

McDowell and Mowl (1995) reported on three collaborative case studies, looking at innovative assessments, carried out at the University of Northumbria. Two involved forms of self and peer assessment of course work and the third an extended group project assessed via a group presentation and written reports. Their findings foreground the need for lecturers to keep in mind basic principles such as fairness in assessments, the need for qualitative feedback, confidence in the objectivity and expertise or authority of markers, and some sense of student control over the assessment process. Where these factors are not present learning gains are compromised. McDowell and Mowls' study is an excellent example of the way in which lessons can be learnt from practitioner research.

Other case studies offer insights into the way in which radical changes in the delivery of courses are received and understood by students, for instance the introduction of the Keller Plan or courses based wholly or partly on learning contracts (Gibbs and Jenkins, 1992).

Students are not, as far as we can tell from the research literature, consulted about changes in course delivery or assessment. Much anxiety is generated by changes which are unfamiliar, not only because they imply unfamiliar routines, but also because they may imply different ideas about knowledge and call for a level of skill (such as interpersonal skills) that students do not yet possess.

A major concern for new lecturers is getting the pitch right. This has its counterpart in the students' overriding concern to bring some order to the learning experience. Research in this area is central to professional concerns, informing methods, and course design.

Hyland (1994) carried out a series of semi-structured interviews with 11 students over the course of their first year, asking them about their experiences of learning. His research confirmed the oft-repeated point that students' concern with assessment overrides other considerations. Assessment directs attention to 'relevant' aspects of the course. Feedback and grades are scrutinized in order to find the 'formula' for doing well. Hyland found evidence of rote learning being adopted as a short-term coping strategy and evidence of changing perspectives on the nature of knowledge, which has been reported by Perry (1970). One conclusion that Hylands draws is that students need help in seeing learning as a process rather than as an initiation into a 'mysterious rite'.

He rightly points to the necessity of developing ways to do this.

This is an important but under-researched area. Finding out how students can be helped to develop more effective learning strategies could start with an investigation into the ones currently being promoted by your courses. A semi-structured interview method could be directed to how students perceive the assessment scheme. You could use such questions such as:

- Do you know how the assessment scheme works?
- How will this understanding inform your learning?
- If you had a say in designing the scheme what would you add or take out?

Large Teaching Groups

Teaching large groups present problems of student anonymity and passivity in learning. It is possible to improve the quality of lectures so that they communicate clearly (Ashcroft and Foreman-Peck, 1994). Gibbs (1992) argues that dealing with large numbers requires either that you increase control over student learning or increase the degree of autonomy students have over their own learning. It is possible to use both approaches, although you will have to be careful that students do not become confused about what is expected of them. (Alternative methods for teaching large groups are described in Ashcroft and Foreman-Peck, 1994). Simply lecturing is, however, widely acknowledged to be ineffective as a main teaching strategy. It may be that a better learning experience for the students could be promoted by the use of carefully structured assessments, including self-assessments, setting small group exercises within the setting of the large group or using interactive handouts. There is a lack of research into effective ways of managing the learning of individuals within large groups.

Interesting research questions could focus around the way in which assessment could be used to promote a sense of active engagement with course content. Self-assessment, for instance can be used as one element of a formal assessment scheme with the intention of promoting deep learning. The research task below gives an example of how you might begin to elicit student perceptions about the affect that the assessment regime of your courses is having on their learning. This could form the first step of an action research project. Robson (1993) discusses general issues involved in designing and carrying out interviews.

RESEARCH TASK. SEMI-STRUCTURED INTERVIEW SCHEDULE

Before beginning the interview you should tell the interviewees that the contents of the interview will not be divulged without permission and that the interviewees' names will not be divulged.

- List the topics that you would like to cover in the interview; for example overall assessment load, the quality of student learning, how self-assessment exercises are regarded.
- List any key questions; for example if the load is experienced as too heavy, how are students coping?
- List a set of associated prompts; these could be examples of what you mean or alternative phrasing.

Since you wish to elicit student perspectives you need to probe their meaning. Here is an example of one item on an interview schedule:

Question	Do you think the assessment load on your course is right?
Prompts	Do you think the amount of assessment is right?
	Do you think that you are asked to do too much for course X?
	Do you think that some course components are under-assessed?
Probes	Why do you think the assessment load is too much/inadequate/satisfactory?
	If you could suggest an improvement to the course team, what would it be?

Summary

In this chapter we have presented some ideas for practitioner research which we believe to be topical and important. In all research endeavours your desire to find out and publish research findings has to be balanced against other considerations. These include respecting other people's right to privacy and the right not to be harmed by your investigations. Evaluations, for example, are potentially very damaging to participants. It is essential therefore that at the start of your research you give serious consideration to these ethical questions. Many institutions have a set of principles, or a code, governing research activity. Before you start any research you should familiarize yourself with your institution's or your profession's code. Ethical principles governing action research need to be carefully considered since there is an element of collaboration.

Robson (1993) presents these in an easy to read format. The next chapter considers collaborative forms of student learning and raises some of the philosophical issues involved in collaboration generally.

Annotated Reading List

Robson, C (1993) *Real World Research: A Resource for social scientists and practitioner researchers*, Oxford: Blackwell.
This is an easy to read and enjoyable introduction to research methods.
Gibbs, G (1995) (ed.) *Improving Student Learning through Assessment and Evaluation*, Oxford: The Oxford Centre for Staff Development, Oxford Brookes University.
This is the second collection of research papers presented at an annual conference held in September by the Oxford Centre for Staff Development. These volumes are well worth acquiring since they contain the most up-to-date reports of practitioner research into teaching, learning and assessment in higher education.

References

Ashcroft, K and Foreman-Peck, L (1994) *Managing Teaching and Learning in Further and Higher Education*, London: Falmer Press.
Ashcroft, K and Palacio, D (1996) *Researching into Assessment and Evaluation in Colleges and Universities*, London: Kogan Page.
Carr, W and Kemmis, S (1986) *Becoming Critical: Education, knowledge and action research*, London: Falmer Press.
DES (1985) *The Development of Higher Education into the 1990s*, Cmnd 9524, London: HMSO.
Elliott, J (1991) *Action Research for Educational Change*, Buckingham: Open University Press.
Elliott, J (1993) 'What have we learned from action research in school-based evaluation?', *Educational Action Research*, 1, 1,175–86.
Elton, L (1994) *Management of Teaching and Learning: Towards change in universities*, London: CVCP/SRHE.
Foreman-Peck, L, Tallantyre, F and Boyne, N (1992) *Six Case Studies of Enterprising Courses at the University of Northumbria in Newcastle*, Newcastle: University of Northumbria at Newcastle.
Fullan, M and Hargreaves, A (1992) *Teacher Development and Educational Change*, London: Falmer Press.
Gibbs, G, Habeshaw, S and Habeshaw, T (1988) *53 Interesting Ways to Appraise your Teaching*, Bristol: Technical and Educational Services.
Gibbs, G and Jenkins, A (eds) (1992) *Teaching Large Classes in Higher Education: How to maintain quality with reduced resource*, London: Kogan Page.

Gibbs, G (1994) *Improving Student Learning: Theory and practice*, Oxford: The Oxford Centre for Staff Development, Oxford Brookes University.

Hyland, R (1994) 'Know the formula and hit the jack pot! First year students on learning', in Gibbs, G (ed.) *Improving Student Learning: Theory and practice*, Oxford: Oxford Centre for Staff Development, Oxford Brookes University.

Landgrebe, B and Winter, R (1994) 'Reflective writing on practice: professional support for the dying?', *Educational Action Research*, 2, 1, 83–95.

Loder, C, Clayton, D, Murray, R, Cox, R and Schofield, A (1989) *Teaching Quality in Higher Education: A review of research and literature*, London: Institute of Education, University of London for the PCFC Committee of Enquiry into Teaching Quality.

McDowell, L and Mowl, G (1995) 'Innovative assessment: its impact on students', in Gibbs,G (ed.) *Improving Student Learning through Assessment and Evaluation*, Oxford: Oxford Centre for Staff Development, Oxford Brookes University.

Marton, F and Saljo, R (1984) 'Approaches to learning' in Marton, F, Hounsell, DJ and Entwistle, NJ (eds) *The Experience of Learning*, Edinburgh: Scottish Academic Press.

Mezirow, J (1981) 'A critical theory of adult learning and education', *Education*, 32, 1, 3–24.

Pendry, A (1990) *The Oxford Internship Scheme: Integration and partnership in initial teacher education*, London: Calouste Gulbenkian Foundation.

Perry, WG (1970) *Intellectual and Ethical Development in the College Years*, New York: Holt, Rinehart, and Winston.

Ramsden, P (1992) *Learning to Teach in Higher Education*, London: Routledge.

Robson, C (1993) *Real World Research: A resource for social scientists and practitioner researchers*, Oxford: Blackwell.

Schwartz, P and Webb, G (1993) *Case Studies on Teaching in Higher Education*, London: Kogan Page.

Sikes, PJ, Measor, L and Woods, P (1985) *Teachers Careers: Conflicts and continuities*, London: Falmer Press.

Taylor, E (1978) 'Orientations to study: A longitudinal interview investigation of students in two human studies degree course at Surrey University', unpublished PhD thesis, Guildford: University of Surrey.

Thomas, D (1995) 'Treasonable or trustworthy text: reflection on teacher narrative studies', in Thomas, D (ed.) *Teachers' Stories*, Buckingham: Open University Press.

Times Higher Educational Supplement (1995) Letters page, 17 February and 24 February.

Titchin, A and Binnie, (1993) 'A unified action research strategy in nursing', *Educational Action Research*, 1, 1, 25–33.

Chapter 3

Researching Collaboration in Teaching and Learning

This chapter explores further the changing professional identity of the lecturer through examining collaborative teaching and learning strategies. We discuss reasons why these strategies may be appropriate and examine some of the pedagogical issues involved. We suggest a number of possible strategies, their implications for assessment, including team work, and resource-based, or open learning as a mode of course delivery. We also discuss the concept of student autonomy, or independence, and how this affects the role of the college or university lecturer. The chapter divides into two sections, each with two research suggestions.

Peer Teaching and Collaboration

Before suggesting some benefits which lecturers can gain from adopting collaborative teaching and learning strategies, we shall examine some of the philosophical assumptions involved. Within adult education especially, there has been a move away from a dissemination, towards a developmental, understanding of and approach to the teaching–learning process (see for example, Boot and Hodgson, 1987; Freire, 1972; Knowles, 1983; Rogers, 1969). This involves learning by doing, learning through experimentation and learning by problem-solving rather than learning by listening to an expert. This also resembles what can be described as an 'open' view of the learning process. Boot and Hodgson (1987) usefully contrast what they call 'two orientations to open learning', namely the dissemination and the development approach. In the dissemination approach, knowledge is regarded as a commodity. It already exists, like something that can be bought and sold. One who owns this commodity can pass it on to those who lack it; in other words, teachers who possess the knowledge transmit it to students who require it. In contrast, the developmental understanding of knowledge regards it as a 'process of engaging with and attributing meaning to the world, including self in it' (p.8). In this view, knowledge is not 'out there', like items in a supermarket to be purchased, but results from a personal process of 'construing meaning'.

The dissemination approach assumes that the teacher or lecturer is an expert. Since they possess knowledge, or the power to decide what qualifies as knowledge, they tend to control the process. What is taught and how it is taught are controlled by the 'guardian of knowledge'. In contrast, the development approach becomes much more collaborative. If knowledge results from a process of engagement with the world, from 'construing meaning', then – according to Boot and Hodgson – teachers' constructions must take their place alongside those of their students. Thus, the 'meanings he/she attributes... [are] no more valid than anyone else's' (p.8). The tutor's role ceases to be that of expert or guardian of knowledge, and becomes instead that of a facilitator. It was Knowles (1983), building on the contribution of Rogers (1969), who popularized the notion of the educator as facilitator rather than as subject expert. Rogers is famous, or infamous, for his remark that:

> Teaching, in my estimation, is a vastly overrated function.
>
> Having made such a statement, I scurry to the dictionary to see if I really mean what I say. Teaching means 'to instruct'. Personally, I am not much interested in instructing another in what she should know or think, though others seem to love to do this. 'To impart knowledge or skill'. My reaction is, why not be more efficient, using a book or programmed learning? 'To make to know'. Here my hackles rise. I have no wish to make anyone know something. 'To show, guide, direct'. As I see it, too many people have been shown, guided, directed. So I came to the conclusion that I do mean what I said. Teaching is, for me, a relatively unimportant and vastly over-valued activity (p.119).

Rogers was using strong language to object, not to teaching as such but rather to a particular understanding of the teaching function. What he was actually reacting against was the concept that teacher knows, and only teacher knows, what is worth knowing. The teacher as facilitator is less an expert in a subject, more an expert in how people learn. Facilitation has its own set of necessary skills; it demands its own expertise. For example, it is the facilitator's responsibility to set the initial mood or climate of the group within which the developmental process can occur. He or she must also be able to advise students on how to access information they need, or on how to conduct, say, field research. Certainly, at postgraduate level, it is by no means unusual for a student to possess a far greater knowledge of their subject than their supervisor does. The supervisor's role is to ensure that students use appropriate research strategies, have thought about alternatives, have identified suitable samples or textual sources, rather than to pass on information about their subject. Rogers identifies ten tasks which learning facilitators are required to fulfil:

1. The good facilitator will create an atmosphere of mutual trust in the classroom.
2. He/she will help clarify individual and group expectations, not fearing possible clashes between individual's freedom to express their objectives.
3. He/she will encourage and enable individuals to pursue their interests/objectives through advice on appropriate courses of study.
4. He/she will make available as wide a range of learning resources as possible.
5. He/she will be flexible in how they allow themselves to be used by the group. They will not 'downgrade' themselves 'as a resource' but neither will they assume a position of superiority.
6. He/she will take students' emotions and feelings into account as well as their intellectual ideas.
7. Increasingly, as the atmosphere of trust is established, the facilitator will become a participant observer – one of the group, 'expressing… views as those of one individual only'.
8. He/she will take initiative in sharing his/her own feelings as well as intellectual ideas with the group.
9. He/she remains alert to student feelings and to any clashes within the group, always attempting to understand what is going on from the individual's point of view.
10. He/she will learn to recognize the limits of his/her own abilities to fulfil these functions.
    (Paraphrase of pp.164–6, *Freedom to Learn*, 1969, Carl Rogers on the learning facilitator.)

Rogers, a counsellor and therapist before he ventured into the field of adult education, is convinced that people learn best when they are able to exercise a measure of control over the learning process. In other words, people need to accept responsibility for their own learning, just as much as they need to accept responsibility for the decisions they make in life. Here we have what others refer to as child- or student-centred learning, or the concept of student/learner autonomy. In adult education, this was proposed as long ago as 1913:

> Discover your own needs, organise in your own way, study as you wish
> to study.... . The initiative must lie with the students. They must say
> how, why, what or when they wish to study. It is the business of their
> colleagues the scholars and administrators to help them obtain the
> satisfaction of their desires
> (Mansbridge, 1913, cited in Jarvis, 1987, p.30).

Obviously, the hierarchical view of the teacher as 'the one who knows
best', and of students as 'those who should do what they are told' is
challenged by this understanding of the educational process. Freire (1972)
contrasts 'banking' education with 'diological' and was fully aware of
the implications of his view for power relationships in the classroom:

> The more students work at storing the deposits entrusted to them, the
> less they develop the critical consciousness which would result from
> their intervention in the world as transformers of that world (p.47).

There are, however, some educationalists who, while recognizing the
importance of an enquiry-based approach, and of learning by doing,
nevertheless argue that the above view tends towards a post-modernist
scepticism about the possibility of 'objective' knowledge. If knowledge
is only what we construe, does it not become totally subjective? Robbins
(1988), for example, accepts as good practice learning by discovery,
experiential learning, and non-directive methods, but is highly critical
of some assumptions which inform present practice in the field. He
argues that the influence of human psychologists, such as Rogers, and
of what he calls 'American pragmatism' has resulted in too radical an
individualism. He remains convinced that there are 'objective things to
be known and that the essence of independent study should be' to
'provide access to that objectivity rather than reduce it to self-knowledge'.
He views the overemphasis on 'individual selectivity of knowledge' as
anti-rational and anti-intellectual. Partially defending an objectivist theory of knowledge, he criticizes the 'paradigm shift attack on the possibility of rational proposals'. His thesis is that 'given what "independent
study" has come to mean' (p.11), namely, 'self-actualization', its liberating
potential has been muted. In his view, 'the alliance between educational
reformism and person-centredness is... undermining' (p.75) potential
for social transformation, democratization and political empowerment.
Rather than reducing the gap between those who possess the 'technical
and practical knowledge necessary to occupy positions of control', it
increases the gap by offering the majority only 'politically impotent,
person-centred, self-development' (p.175).

Robbins also strikes a cautious note about political realism; it is, he says, 'naive' to think that the type of negotiation which Knowles and others regard as crucial to good adult education practice, 'could be anything other than reflections of unequal power relations' (p.157) given that, at the end of the day, tutors are accountable to examination boards and to university or college committees for the performance of their students. Boot and Hodgson's concept of tutors' voices carrying no more weight or authority than their students' may be impossible to practise if syllabuses are to be delivered and academic standards maintained. There may also be sound pedagogical or even ethical reasons, sometimes, for tutor intervention when students, exercising choice of control, make decisions which the tutor wishes to challenge. For example, one of the authors of this book recently allowed students to form their own teams to work together on a topic, selected from the syllabus, of their own choice. All overseas (exchange) students ended up in one group; all those from minority backgrounds in another. Such segregation, in the tutor's view, was unhealthy and, perhaps especially for the overseas students, would prevent the very exchange of experiences and contexts which their programme is designed to facilitate. The tutor thus needs to reserve a modicum of control, although this can be exercised in a non-directive style, for example, through discussion and dialogue about aims, objectives and programme goals.

When are Collaborative Strategies Appropriate?

Robbins critique of a view which makes all knowledge subjective has already introduced a note of caution into this discussion of collaborative learning strategies. We should be aware that collaborative strategies are not always appropriate and that careful thought is required about *why* we want to employ them before we do so. Practically, as suggested above, few degree or diploma syllabi in colleges and universities allow total student control, either over the mechanics of a course (when it is taught, what assignments tasks are set, when they have to be submitted) or in the construction of meaning. Most disciplines, while open to new concepts, to new or to different interpretations have basic building blocks of information without which their frontiers can not be extended. On the other hand, once basic rules, methodological issues, and standard theories in any given discipline have been introduced, collaborative learning strategies – in which students can test, apply or develop these – may then become appropriate. In contrast to a traditional lecture (which almost by definition represents a dissemination strategy, and is hierarchical) collaborative strategies are participatory, active and democratic.

Elsewhere (see, for example, Chapter 4), we contrast 'surface' with 'deep' learning. Participatory, problem solving learning tends to result in deep learning – learning which becomes integrated into the student's own experience. This is probably the most powerful educational argument for adopting these strategies. Other reasons in favour of adopting these strategies can also be identified. We have already discussed some of the pedagogical problems associated with increased class sizes, including the difficulty of using interactive teaching/learning techniques. Peer teaching and team work can help solve this problem. It may release tutors' time for personal research, or for producing resource-based learning materials, although whether either actually happens may itself be a suitable research question. Both as a response to increased class sizes, and as a rational way of using human and material resources, many institutions are investing in resource-based and open learning, which we discuss below (and also in Chapter 5). This, though, requires staffing: use of peer-teaching/team work strategies are relatively cheap in terms of staffing costs.

As indicated above, these strategies will be more appropriate for particular stages of any given curriculum. An example from one of the authors' own experience may prove useful: generally, he tries to make much wider use of peer-teaching/team work in delivering second- or third-year courses than in year one of a Bachelors degree on which he teaches. Year one introduces methodological issues within the subject, and applies these to a range of topics. The tutor does include some interactive work but he tends to retain control over this himself. However, by year two, students have become familiar with methodology and – if somewhat passively – they have also seen this applied. Now, in student-led teams, they can apply the same methodological techniques to a different range of topics. Having, in year one, picked up some of the essential building blocks of information about 'belief systems', they now explore how these are brought into dialogue with contemporary issues. Because the topics discussed are contemporary, a great deal of the most up-to-date and relevant data are in journals and newspapers, rather than in books. Often, the debate is moving on almost daily. The tutor does not claim to be able to keep ahead of the whole range of issues and debates which are covered by the course, nor would it be a good use of time to attempt to do so. On the other hand, student teams, each working on a different topic, can access CD-ROMs, write to relevant bodies, and engage in hands-on research such as field work, interviews and visits. This strategy may very well result in a genuine learning– teaching partnership between students and the tutor, in which, as Freire says, 'Teachers are no longer those who "teach", but those who are themselves "taught" in dialogue with the students, who in turn while being taught also teach. They become jointly responsible for a process in which all grow' (cited in Rogers, 1969, p.81). A practical benefit for the tutor of this approach is that they can make use of the information provided by students in their own research and publications. This, of course, ought to be fully acknowledged, else one might very well be accused of plagiarizing one's students' work.

What Strategies Can Be Used?

There are different strategies involved in peer teaching and in collaborative learning. One obvious example of peer teaching is when we make occasional use of a student in our class who has, because of their background, relevant experience in a particular area. This could be communicated through a traditional lecture, or by leading a seminar discussion. When discussing a certain issue, several members of the class may have relevant experience, and can lead small buzz-group sessions which feed into a tutor-led plenary. Finding out what students bring to any given course at the beginning can suggest opportunities for employing peer teaching. For example, on a course on ethics taught by one of the authors, some students have teaching backgrounds, some medical, some commercial, some clerical. Others have volunteered in hospices, sheltered housing projects, and so on. Many will have had first-hand experience of thinking through ethical problems, and of acting on their decisions. Here are rich resources for leading sessions during the course.

Team work, though, is probably the most universally applicable strategy because it does not depend on the rather random presence, or absence, of experienced individuals. It is, as indicated above, especially appropriate when students are researching contemporary issues or applying methodology. It can usefully be linked to project work, and this can easily serve as the assessed element of the course. This may or may not involve peer assessment. The project might lead to a presentation, to an exhibition, or to a folder of work containing a number of different items. If different teams are researching/exploring different topics, the presentation and/or exhibition made or mounted will also be a form of peer teaching, as each group benefits from each others' work.

Another strategy which facilitates student autonomy and ability to control the learning process is the learning contract. There is now a considerable body of literature about the concept and use of learning contracts, for example, ranging over the decade from Knowles (1983) to Cork (1993). Learning contracts consist of an agreement between the course provider and students about what they will do, when they will do it, and how their performance will be assessed, or as Knowles writes, 'what will be learned, how it will be learned, when it will be learned, and if it has to be learned' (Knowles, 1983, p.52). Some programmes may be able to allow an almost unlimited amount of student choice over these aspects – generally if they do not have to meet rigid completion deadlines. It is, though, unlikely that any programme using learning packages will be able to afford this degree of student control. Probably, if total student control is a possibility, the programme will be skill- or competency-based, consisting of a series of tasks which students have to complete, and produce evidence of competency. The NVQ (National Vocational Qualification) portfolio, for example, consists of 'evidence from the workplace to show they [students] have met the competencies for that level laid down in the standards' (Ashcroft and Foreman-Peck, 1994, p.63). This does not usually allow much choice about which tasks are to be completed.

Most course providers will have to set an outside deadline within which proof of achievement must be produced if a student is to gain the award. However, even in three-year degree programmes there may be scope for learning contracts, especially if they relate to task-oriented assessment or assignments. For example, if certain data-collecting, laboratory experiments, or field work skills are involved, students could negotiate which tasks they will perform at a given stage, leading to the full schedule of tasks being completed at the end of their final year. This, as suggested, could include some choice from a menu of relevant tasks. Tutor supervision of student team project work, if the project is to be carried out over a lengthy period, could also involve negotiating goals and timetable. Gosling (1993) describes how informal learning contracts can be used to encourage the development of seminar skill capabilities.

Pedagogical Issues and Problems

The most obvious problems arise from the different learning-teaching experience which student-led team work involves. For the students, there is the challenge of managing their own time, of sharing tasks and responsibilities, of being responsible for finding their own material. Used to this being disseminated by the tutor, they now have to locate resources for themselves. Concern often emerges about whether individual performances will be adversely affected; in other words, will a strong student be pulled down by a member of the team failing to pull their weight. Safeguards will need to be put in place. Each student might produce a separate learning log, or journal, recording the amount of time spent on the project, assessing their own contribution, and commenting on that of others. This, of course, may create a climate of mutual suspicion. Perhaps an agreed assessment of each others' contribution would be more democratic. It might be pointed out that the skill of working as an equal member of a team is an important life-skill, and that whether we like it or not, difficult decisions about other people's contributions have to be made. A strategy which can help individuals' take responsibility for their own contributions (which can also enable them to help others contribute) is for one member to be a 'scrutineer'. He or she will act as a participant observer. Instead of contributing directly to the discussion, they will observe the roles played by each member of the team, and note who dominates at the expense of others, who finds it difficult to make themselves heard, who goes off at a tangent, who makes connections which help the group progress towards achieving its goals, etc. Peer assessment of presentations or projects can also be made – tutors need to provide criteria. Tutors may wish to reserve the right to differentiate between individual marks within a team, depending on evidence provided by the learning logs. Alternatively, teams may distribute the mark amongst their members according to their own assessment of individual roles.

Given their increased responsibility, perhaps including self- or peer assessment, students may resent the tutor's use of this strategy. Is he or she not the expert? Does he or she not *know* what the project is worth? Why should they be expected to do the tutor's job? The tutor may feel liberated to use time for personal research, leaving students to look after themselves. However, the tutor remains responsible for the learning experience, if not for the learning process. It is part of his or her role as facilitator to ensure that students are properly inducted into a team work mode of learning. He or she will need to offer advice on target setting, and on group organization. They will need to clarify and make explicit the aims and objectives of the project, and the assessment criteria. They will need to offer initial advice on where resources might be located, or make their field contacts available. They will need to observe team meetings, thus assuring students that they are picking up any problems and are available to assist when necessary. They will also need to guard against advantaging one team by offering it more help than another. One way of utilizing the time available is as follows. Assume that a two-hour session (lecture followed by seminar) has been timetabled. During the first half hour, all teams and tutor can meet. Each team can update the whole group on its progress, mentioning any particular problems or achievements. Tutor offers encouragement, advice – or admonition! In the next half hour, the tutor briefly visits each group. In the second hour, the tutor makes him or herself available in their study for consultation – meanwhile, engaging in other tasks!

Another possible student anxiety is over whether they are adequately covering the curriculum. There is a danger that their presentations or projects will contain a lot of data or relevant material but lack analyses. They may find the transition from mainly passive to participatory learning too daunting. A phased-in strategy can be used; formative assessment based on a team work project, for which one out of the two scheduled hours is used; with summative assessment by traditional essay or examination related to a series of lectures using the other hour available.

Research Issues

There are some interesting research issues here, related both to student and to tutor experience of different teaching/learning strategies. How do students respond to a change in teaching/learning mode? Are the anxieties mentioned above, or others, part of their response? For example, do weaker students 'pull down' the stronger, or do stronger students 'pull up' the weaker; indeed do different strengths and weaknesses emerge? What new skills are students aware of needing/acquiring? What new skills does the tutor develop, or identify the need to develop? What do students think about the changed role of the tutor? What similarities/differences emerge between students' assessment of their progress, and the tutor's? Is this approach less, or more demanding, on the tutor? Does it actually liberate any time for personal research? Does the scrutineer strategy work? Were their comments/role resented, appreciated? Did they feel that their contribution was worthwhile?

If used, learning logs or journals can provide data to illuminate some of the above. A discussion or evaluation session at the end of the course can usefully explore many of the above issues. Do students feel that the aims and objectives were met? Were they clear? Did they understand the assessment criteria? Did they feel that the marks were fairly awarded? How did they respond to the tutor's role? What improvements would they suggest for next year's group? What skills do they think they developed? How would they compare the experience with a more traditional course delivery? Do students think that this type of approach would not work for certain subjects or topics? Do they think it would work better for some than for others? If, in the light of your findings, you are able to implement changes to course delivery, you may have completed the first phase of a possible action research cycle.

A research project could focus on tutor and student experience of a new learning-teaching mode. A preliminary task would be to identify which aspect of the course might be suitable for a team-work, project-based approach. You might consult colleagues to identify elements of the course which require a deep approach and those which require a surface approach. The task suggested by Ashcroft and Foreman-Peck (1994, p.42) could be used. Obviously, feelings and emotions will play a large part in how students and staff perceive the success, or failure, of any innovation; therefore, a qualitative approach is appropriate. The tutor and a selected number of students willing to participate in the project could all keep journals. These should contain a record of their feelings about their changed role, about others' roles within the group, and an assessment of the learning experience. As Bell (1993) points out, it is essential for the success of this research strategy that participants are fully in 'sympathy with the task... reluctant subjects will rarely provide usable data' (p.102). The benefit to participants of gaining a deeper understanding about the learning process itself may offset reluctance to spend time on the task.

RESEARCH TASK. RESEARCH DIARIES: 1

There are at least two ways of using journals.

1. You may ask participants to respond to some specific issues, or questions, such as:

- How much time did you spend today working on the project?
- Do you think that all members of the team are contributing equally to the project?
- Do you think that the aims and objectives of the course are clearly understood by members of your team?
- Do you like/dislike this way of working?
- Do you think it an easy option for the tutor?
- Do you think the tutor is offering enough guidance?
- Which different skills are you aware of developing?

2. Instead of prejudging which issues might be involved, you can ask participants to record, in their own words, their reactions to and feelings about the course. The advantage of the former is that analysis is easier when the categories are predetermined; the advantage of the latter is that the issues and questions will be generated from out of the journals themselves. There may be issues which you did not anticipate. Thus, the analytical framework will emerge from the data, instead of from your predetermined set of issues. This is sometimes referred to in the literature on research as 'grounded theory'. Neuman (1994, p.322) writes:

> A quantitative researcher gathers data after he theorizes, develops hypotheses, and creates measures or variables. By contrast, a qualitative researcher begins with a research question and little else. Theory develops during the data collection process. This more inductive method means that theory is built from data or grounded in the data.

The research question here is 'How do staff and students experience a new learning-teaching mode?' Subsidiary questions ask which factors, positive and negative, can be identified as having contributed to the learning or teaching process.

The research will itself show what issues are significant, which may or may not resemble those which we have suggested in this chapter. In analysing the journals, the so-called 'critical incident' and 'portfolio' approaches may prove useful. The object of the exercise is to identify factors which hinder participants benefiting from the learning-teaching mode, and factors which facilitate this. This approach assumes that work, in this case team work, project or presentation preparation, involves critical and non-critical tasks. A 'critical task might be defined as one which makes the difference between success and failure', and the idea, says Bell (1994), is to 'collect reports as to what people do that is particularly effective in contributing to good performance' (p.106). Similarly, the 'problem portfolio' records 'information about how each problem arose, methods used to solve it, difficulties encountered and so on' (p.106). In other words, what problems did teams encounter; how did they resolve them; what worked well; what did not work well?

Comparison of staff and students' journals should identify similarities and differences between their respective perceptions of the learning-teaching process. It may be useful to begin the research with a session for all participants on keeping reflective journals. For example, the following schema could be adapted:

Column 1: Notes place, time, people present, nature of interaction (eg, team meeting), agrees topic.

Column 2: Notes inferences, eg, Sally seems to have dominated the discussion, James seems to resent this.

Column 3: Analyses, eg, group needs to work at mechanism for arriving at consensus.

Column 4: Personal reflection, eg, I didn't really express my own opinion either! Tutor didn't help much.

(Adapted from Neuman, 1994, p.353).

Burgess (1984) contains material on research diaries, including suggestions for their design and lay-out, and their usefulness for research.

After analysing the data gathered from the journals, you could meet with the whole student group to use the nominal group technique (outlined in Chapter 2) to check whether the results of your journal analysis match the experience of those who did not take part in the journal exercise. Later in this chapter we summarize steps and procedures in analysing data.

RESEARCH TASK. RESEARCH DIARIES: 2

Are the claims we make about teaching-learning strategies which encourage surface or deep learning justified? Do they achieve what we think they do? It is rarely possible in qualitative research to attempt a controlled experiment, unlike research scientists who often treat one patient with one drug, another with a different drug, and observe the results. However, it might be possible to conduct research simultaneously into two different teaching-learning modes. Students involved in both might record, in their journals, their own perceptions of the advantages and disadvantages of the different modes. The disadvantage of this is that it makes an additional demand on students – to cooperate with your research.

An alternative research strategy would be to compare results of any summative assessment attached to either mode – a lecture series, or assessed team work. Does the former indicate that surface learning, the latter that deep learning, has resulted from the respective teaching-learning modes? This research could itself be conducted by a staff team. First, indicators of surface and of deep learning will need to be agreed. Staff could begin by writing down, independently, which indicators they believe can be used to assess the depth of a student's learning. Group negotiation could then decide which indicators are the most significant, and result in an agreed list being compiled.

- First, check which indicators of performance have been identified by several, or all, colleagues. Ask whether anyone who did not identify them wants to argue strongly against its usefulness.
- Second, ask whether anyone whose choice of a performance indicator was not on other people's lists want to argue strongly in its favour.
- Next, each staff member would independently assess student work, applying their agreed criteria, then correlate their results.

Such a team approach also 'offers the opportunity for researcher triangulation' (Hammersley and Atkinson, 1995, p.231). Talbot's (1994) 'Learning journals for evaluation of group-based learning' also provides some useful material.

Open and Resource-based Learning

Team work, as described above, gives students an increased measure of independence and responsibility, as well as encouraging them to use and share their own experiences. Team work, if project-related, is also an example of resource-based learning. In as much as student team and project work involves use of IT and of library resources independently of the tutor, it is resource-based. Usually, though, the term 'resource-based' is used to describe the delivery of whole courses via learning packages, which may consist of video and/or audio-tapes as well as printed material. Use of such learning packs features prominently within the delivery of open and distant learning programmes when, to a large extent, they serve as a substitute for the face-to-face lecture. Instead of the necessary building blocks of information being dissemi-nated by the teacher, they are disseminated in this prepackaged form.

What are Open and Distant Learning?

The Open University delivers its courses through learning packs and associated television and radio programmes. Students work through the material individually, usually at home. Holmberg (1995) concludes that despite increased use of information technology, 'There is no change in the basic conditions: students still mainly study individually…' (p.49). Students may not, in developmental terms, actually exercise very much autonomy while using such packages. The questions contained in the learning packs may be designed to elicit set, preconceived, or narrowly defined responses. There may be very little flexibility over choice of topics, or over assignment tasks, or in their ability to control the timetable. This, indeed, is the case with most Open University courses which, says Rowntree (1992), have fairly rigid timetables and assessment schedules.

There has been considerable debate about the meaning of the now widely used term 'open learning', including a famous debate between two Open University professors, Rumble and Lewis. In their respective articles, both published in the *Open Learning* journal, they disagreed about the definition of 'openness'. Rumble (1989) took this to refer to universal access, and accused programmes which describe themselves as 'part of an open learning programme' but whose entry is restricted, of misleading advertising. Lewis (1990) in his reply, pointed out that initial openness to anyone may have 'little point' if, once enrolled, 'choice is restricted at almost every point', and that 'open learning' is 'not so much associated with access as with widening the choice over the content of the curriculum' (p.5). Lewis also argued that, in practice, openness will 'lie somewhere on a spectrum' – it will be a process that can be measured on a 'closed-open continuum'. An appropriate question, then, is 'Which aspects' of a given programme 'should be open for this target group and by how much?' (p.8).

Rowntree (1992, p.20), adopting Lewis' concept of a closed-open continuum, offers a useful checklist to measure 'openness'. He asks:

'WHO can learn?'
How easy is it for someone to become a learner without restrictions of age, qualification, wealth, job, etc...

and 'WHAT do they learn?'
To what extent is the learner free to decide the content and objectives of the programme and when and how he or she will be assessed?

and 'HOW do they learn?'
To what extent is the learner free to decide where, when and at what pace he or she will learn, the teaching/learning methods to use and the routes to take, and how he or she will call on other people for support?

Lewis (1990, p.8) also suggests that the question, 'Which aspects' of a given programme 'should be open for this target group and by how much?' is an appropriate consideration.

In addition to these two understandings of openness – as universal access and as control over content, assessment and timetable – a third view can be identified. This associates openness with the degree to which students are enabled to 'engage with and attribute meaning to the world, including self in it' (Boot and Hodgson, 1987, p.8).

Open learning, then, delivered via resource-packages, may or may not enable learner autonomy as this is understood by the development/process orientation to learning. Some educationalists think that programmes which do not encourage learner autonomy should not qualify as open, but should only be described as 'distant'. Field (1994), for example, takes distant learning to refer to programmes which are delivered 'at a distance' via learning packages, while the designation 'open' should only apply to programmes which aim to promote learner autonomy. He writes:

> As a philosophy, open learning implies greater accessibility, flexibility and student centredness: it implies placing learner rather than provider at the core of educational practice (p.3).

Advantages and Disadvantages of Resource-based/Open Learning Strategies

Before employing resource-based or open learning strategies, the advantages and disadvantages of the various modes available require careful consideration. First, what options might we consider? One option is the type of resource-based, open learning-oriented team work approach which we have already described. This may not, in all aspects, qualify as 'open' along the closed-open continuum, but it does, as we have demonstrated, enhance students' ability to take responsibility for the learning process. It also has the advantage of only costing the tutors' normal allocation of hours (even if it may prove not to have the advantage of actually releasing tutor time). It uses existing resources within, or outside, the institute. Other forms of resource-based learning demand investment in purchasing or producing material. For example, instead of a tutor delivering a weekly lecture covering a given topic, a set text, or a pack written by the tutor may be used as a substitute. This, however, depending on the size of the group, may be very expensive. The cost of writing, printing and acquiring copyright permission is unlikely to prove attractive compared with a traditional face-to-face lecture.

This mode of delivery, though, may be more appropriate for fully-funded, part-time students if production costs can be covered by their fees. Even so, before launching a programme, careful costing will be necessary. How will time needed for writing the material be released, for example? Will new staff be employed, will existing staff be redeployed, or encouraged to free-up time by facilitating student-led teaching? Is there a market for the course, and at the price needed to make it financially viable? Rowntree (1992) is written as if it were an open learning text (and is used as a text for an Open University course) and contains useful checklists to guide a prospective provider through each stage of course design and delivery, including the costing process.

Pragmatic Advantages

If you do embark on delivering an open learning course through staff-written materials and study guides, there may be some research benefit involved in this process. First, even if you base what you write on existing lecture notes, you will find yourself updating your materials, which in turn feeds back into your in-house teaching. You may find that the need to produce text encourages you towards innovation and creativity in your field, with obvious research benefit. You may draw on what you have produced in your own publications. There are, however, some serious problems here. First, there is the problem of copyright. What we produce for our institutions becomes institutional property, and is institutional copyright. Most institutions, though, will allow us to use our own material (which remains our intellectual property) for research publications. These contribute to departmental research ratings, while course materials do not. However, course materials are often team products, so we may not be credited with the specific section we want to use for our research article. Sometimes, too, writers are anonymous. A problem might arise here if anyone challenges our claim to the material in question. This may seem unlikely, but it could happen and perhaps the best strategy to prevent this is for authorship to be acknowledged by the Institution. Attribution does not affect copyright.

Pedagogical Issues

Some of the pedagogical issues involved in delivering open learning programmes will have practical or financial implications. Different issues, too, arise depending on which understanding of 'openness' is claimed for the programme we offer. For example, if 'universal access' is taken to qualify our programme as 'open', after Rumble (1989), we will need to decide how to cater for students starting the course with various levels of experience, with different academic skills, and so on. Even programmes which do not have universal access are likely to attract students from a wide range of backgrounds, and at different levels of competence. Members of this writing team have taught groups in which some students have no formal academic qualifications while others possess doctorate degrees. (One member of this writing team has actually been taught by another!) Pragmatically, do we produce different materials for different students? This has obvious cost implications. Do we give some students credit for prior learning, and if so how do we evaluate this? Do such students enter the course at a more advanced point? How do we assess performance when student abilities vary? Do we measure each student in terms of their own progress, from their own starting point? If so, what consequences does this have for our validation and examining procedures?

If we view our programme's openness in terms of student ability to choose content, negotiate assessment and timetable, pragmatic consequences also follow. For example, does their ability to choose content require us to produce a range of different units, and can we afford this? Does their freedom to negotiate assessment and timetable create any difficulty for marking assignments? How flexible can we be, in terms of validation agreements, and given the frequency of examination board meetings? The issue, too, about how much choice or flexibility is desirable for these students at this stage of the programme raises its own pedagogical problematic if we are attempting to be democratic, and view learning as a teacher-student partnership. If tutors decide on the degree of choice, are they not upholding the hierarchical model of teacher authority which the very concept of student autonomy seeks to counteract? We may well recall here Robbins' (1988) cautious note about 'political realism': it is 'naive' to think that negotiation between staff and students 'could be anything other than reflections of unequal power relations' (p.157).

If we identify our programme's openness with student ability to freely construe meanings, to 'engage with and attribute meaning to the world, including self in it', we will need to ensure that course materials are written in a style which reflects this epistemology. This is quite a subtle point but, for example, they will need to demonstrate awareness of alternative viewpoints within their discipline area, and will need to adopt a problem solving, enquiring approach which makes it clear that there are a range of possible responses. Materials, like lecturers, can easily suggest that one viewpoint is preferred by the writer or lecturer, who happens to hold that view him or herself. Exploring whether materials do or do not uphold this concept of openness may be an interesting area for research.

A major pedagogical issue involved in either resource-based or open learning provision is how to build in the type of group work interaction which Lindeman, as far back as 1926, called the ideal 'setting for adult education, the modern quest for life's meaning' (p.7). There is no easy answer to this. Use of computer networking or telephone conferencing may be the answer, although financial implications loom large. These may be beyond the reach of our students. Regional meetings require staffing, as do residential schools. There is much less of a problem if resource-based, open learning provision is college-based, involving full-time students. Even if students work through packages as individuals, they can meet weekly or fortnightly with a tutor. Given the cost of providing each individual student with a package, which could easily rule this out as an in-house delivery mode, an alternative would be for a group of students to work through the material as a team. Each might work though a section at a time, then lead a weekly group discussion. This, of course, also introduces peer teaching, which does not usually feature in this type of delivery mode.

Research Issues

There is a great deal of research involved, by way of producing a feasibility study and business plan, before open learning can be deployed. Once running, many aspects of course design and delivery become suitable subjects for teacher research. Lack of face-to-face contact will clearly make some research strategies less easy to use – observation, for example. Interviews may also be difficult to arrange. One can sit in on in-house student learning teams and observe how they organize themselves – but even attending regional meetings of non-residential students may not be all that easy. A questionnaire is probably the most obvious tool, which does raise the problem of triangulating results. Some telephone interviewing may well be necessary.

What issues might we research? As with the use of team-work strategies within college, some comparative study comparing student experience of an open learning programme with their experience of a traditionally delivered programme, might prove possible. If students have experience of another distant or open learning programme, you may wish to research how their experiences of these compare. This may be of special interest if the aims and objectives, or understanding of openness, of the other course are similar – or indeed different – to those of your own. If a course claims to offer a high degree of student choice and control, do students perceive that this is so? If a course claims to develop students as autonomous learners, are they aware of being so developed and how do they actually experience this? Can they identify skills, competences, an increase in self-confidence, for example?

As with team work in college, so with distant/open learning: students and tutors will each experience their own frustrations. Students may want more contact with/feedback from tutors. Course materials may leave them with unanswered questions. They may feel that the course fails to live up to the claims it makes for itself. Tutors may feel too isolated from their students.

RESEARCH TASK. QUESTIONNAIRE (OPEN)

A similar strategy to the one suggested above for evaluating team work could be adapted to research student experience of the programme. A questionnaire could be used to identify positive and negative aspects, for example:

- What do students like, dislike?
- What do they think enhances their learning?
- What do they think hinders their learning?

This type of questionnaire invites open responses, as opposed to closed ones – for example, a 'yes' or 'no' option.

With questionnaires (including this type of open questionnaire), it is impossible not to ask specific questions, even if they are designed to elicit information which the respondents are not aware they are providing! This always runs the danger, however carefully the questionnaire is designed, of manipulating responses to confirm your own theory or impression. To check the reliability of responses, a limited number of students could be asked to keep a journal. They should not be aware of the questions in the questionnaire, but asked to record their positive and negative experience of the learning process. The information provided by these journals could then be compared with the questionnaire responses. Frequency of reference to particular aspects, for example negative comments about the role of tutors, quality of course materials, or positive comments about these, can be noted. Here are some hints on how to put your data to good use.

Steps in Data Analysis

1. Initially, group data in response to your original research questions (which may be a single question, with subsidiaries). Some data may relate to more than one research question. This

step will help you to create a broad overview of the responses (provided by either a questionnaire, or a journal).

2. Next, examine what has emerged so far to see if any particular pattern (or patterns) has emerged. Also look to see if there are any sub-patterns. Look for similarities; negative and positive comments (for example, what aids/hinders learning, positive or negative comments about the role of the tutor, or about the course materials) should be coded. Also code any data which refuses to fit into any of the patterns – anomalies may be significant; create a separate category for these. In other words, note variety and diversity of opinion around common features and also anything which doesn't seem to fit.

3. Identify patterns in terms of who says what – for example, men, women, older students, younger students, students or staff, etc.

4. What is absent in the data may be significant. What did you expect to find, but did not? Think back, to remind yourself why you had thought it would be significant. Think about whether it is absent from the data because you were mistaken about its importance, or whether your respondents may have had any reason to withhold comment on this aspect. Do you need to pursue this further (follow up with an interview)?

5. Now make explicit the categories you have used to code the data. You may find it useful to show your categories, and some data, to a colleague to see if they think you have done justice to the material.

Procedures. If you are using a manual system (rather than IT; for the use of IT in qualitative analyses, see the Appendix) the following will prove useful: large sheets of paper, coloured pens, highlighters or markers. Use one sheet to correlate your research issues with the data; that is, to create the broad overview referred to in step 1 above. Use another to list your sub-divisions (patterns and sub-patterns), another for matching responses with respondents, and so on. Also record any quotable quotes which you may want to include in your final research report. This physical process will make your codes or categories explicit and help you to satisfy a claim to reliability.

Remember the following ground rules:

● Data analysis must always involve interpreting your material, not merely describing it.
● Interpretation must be systematic and reliable.

- Analysis must reflect patterns embedded in the data; readers must be able to see how your codes or categories are related to or derived from the data.

RESEARCH TASK. EVALUATION EXERCISE

Your research question could focus on the issue of student autonomy, or on whether the understanding of openness which the providers claim for the programme is matched by student experience of the programme.

Stage 1: Analyse course documents and publicity materials to identify the claims made about openness in its promotional literature.

Stage 2: Interview colleagues about their understanding of open learning. Be careful to interview both senior and junior colleagues so that a range of experience is represented within your sample.

Stage 3: Use a questionnaire to find out whether students' perceptions of the programme as open match how staff think it qualifies as open.

Appropriate questions might be:

- Do students consider themselves able to 'control' the learning process?
- Is there enough choice?
- How do they perceive the programme's understanding of what it means to know, or to learn, within the subject or discipline being studied?

Summary

In this chapter we continued our exploration of the changing role of the college and university lecturer as expert in students' learning, rather than as subject experts with a discussion about collaborative and resource-based learning, both of which build on this understanding of the teaching-learning process. We looked at theoretical and pragmatic aspects of collaborative teaching and resource-based teaching and learning, and suggested several possible topics for research in this area. In Chapter 4, we begin by noting that as well as this emphasis on lecturers as experts in how people learn, there is also increased pressure to vocationalize the curriculum, or to skill students for future employment. This has consequences both for how we understand our role, that is, our sense of professional identity, and for how we regard the subjects or disciplines which we teach. Two innovative methods of course delivery

– resource-based learning (as discussed in this chapter), and use of IT
– are often advanced as exemplifying vocational values, as skilling
students for the workplace, and as enabling students to develop as
autonomous learners. Chapter 4 examines how these innovations may
impact on how we understand our own role, as lecturers, and on how
we understand our academic disciplines.

Annotated Reading List and References

Ashcroft, K A and Foreman-Peck, L (1994) *Managing Teaching and Learning in Further and Higher Education*, London: Falmer Press.
Addresses issues faced by teachers in managing teaching and learning drawing throughout on the notion of the reflective practitioner and contains suggested enquiry tasks related to the issues discussed.

Bell, J (1994) *Doing Your Research Project: A guide for first-time researchers in education and social science*, 2nd edn, Buckingham: Open University Press.
A research handbook on planning and conducting research, including how to collect and analyse data. There are useful checklists, for example, on designing questionnaire and interview schedules.

Bennett, C (1995) 'Challenging conventions: An evaluation case study of an open theology degree', unpublished MEd thesis, University of Oxford.
Explores the philosophy and practice of open learning and researches how students experience openness on a distance learning programme.

Boot, R and Hodgson, V (1987) 'Open learning: meaning and experience', in Hodgson, V, Mann, S and Snell, R (eds) *Beyond Distance Teaching: Towards open learning*, Buckingham: Open University Press, pp.5–15.
This chapter contrasts dissemination with developmental methods of teaching, arguing that the latter encourages critical engagement with the learning process, while the former requires only a passive acquisition of facts.

Burgess, R (1984) 'Keeping a research diary', in Bell, J (ed.) *Conducting Small Scale Investigations in Educational Management*, London: Harper and Row, pp.198–205.
Describes how to design, use and analyse both researcher and informants' or participants' research diaries, suggesting division into substantive, methodological and analytical accounts.

Cork, A (1993) *Learning Contracts*, Leicester: De Montfort University.
Part of a self-study pack series, contains a pro forma for designing learning contracts.

Field, J (1994) 'Open learning and consumer culture', *Open Learning*, 9, 2, 3–11.
This article explores links between open learning's student-centred philosophy, and the contemporary demand for consumer choice.

Friere, P (1972) *Pedagogy of the Oppressed*, Harmondsworth: Penguin.
Contrasts a 'banking' approach to teaching and learning with a
'dialogical' approach and sees the former as imprisoning, the latter as
empowering. Written from a Marxist Christian perspective.

Gosling, D (1993) 'Informal learning contracts for skills development', in
Stephenson, J and Laycock, M (eds) (1993) *Using Learning Contracts in
Higher Education*, London: Kogan Page, pp.57–69.
Gosling explores the use of informal contracts between tutors and
students in helping students to develop and enhance their seminar skills.

Hammersley, M and Atkinson, P (1995) *Ethnography: Principles in practice*, 2nd
edn, London: Routledge.
Discusses most aspects of conducting ethnographic research, including
recording and analysing as well as ethical issues and the notion of
reflexivity. It also explores the problematics of both insider and outsider
research.

Holmberg, B (1995) 'The evolution of the character and practice of distance
and open learning', *Open Learning*, 10, 2, 47–53.
A useful summary of developments and trends in open and distance
learning arguing that despite the use of information technology to
improve tutor-student communications, students still work as individuals.

Jarvis, J (ed.) (1987) *Twentieth Century Thinkers in Adult Education*,
Beckenham: Croom Helm.
Different chapters explore such themes as the link between adult
education and social action; the importance of democracy and dialogue;
education for empowerment and the centrality of the adult learner's own
experience.

Knowles, M (1983) *The Adult Learner: A Neglected Species*, Houston: Gulf
Publishing.

Lewis, R (1990) 'Open learning and the misuse of language: A response to
Greville Rumble', *Open Learning*, 5, 1, 3–8.
In this now classic article, Lewis challenges the view that openness is only
to be understood as universal access, arguing instead for openness as
student choice and control over the learning process.

Lindeman, E (1926) *The Meaning of Adult Education*, New York: Republic.
This pioneer work on adult education anticipates many of the current
emphases on learning by doing, participation and democracy.

Neuman, W L (1994) *Social Research Methods: Qualitative and quantitative
approaches*, 2nd edn, Boston, MA: Allyn and Baker.
A very detailed research handbook addressing issues of theory and
practice. Summary 'tables' and 'review questions' help the reader to
engage critically with the text.

Robbins, D (1988) *The Rise of Independent Study: The politics and philosophy of an
educational innovation*, 1970–87, Buckingham: Open University Press.
Interacts with the contributions of Carl Rogers, Malcolm Knowles and
other adult educators, and argues that instead of enabling students to
engage critically with rational propositions, independent study has

become captive to an overly personalistic, anti-rational and anti-intellectual epistemology.

Rogers, C (1969) *Freedom to Learn*, Columbus, OH: Charles E Merrill.
Argues that adults learn best when they can control the learning process. Tutors ought to be facilitators of others' learning, rather than subject experts.

Rowntree, D (1992) *Exploring Open and Distance Learning*, London: Kogan Page.
Written in the format of an Open University course book, and used as such for an Open University unit, this book is a comprehensive discussion of theory and practice. It employs the reflective practitioner model.

Rumble, G (1989) 'Open learning, distance learning and the misuse of language', *Open Learning*, 4, 2, 28–36.
Adopts the Open University's policy of universal access as the sole criterion for openness, and criticizes many restricted access programmes for claiming to be open.

Stephenson, J and Laycock, M (eds) (1993) *Using Learning Contracts in Higher Education*, London: Kogan Page.
A very useful book about learning contracts. The chapter by the editors on 'The place and potential of learning contracts' (pp.159-77) is especially relevant to the focus of this chapter.

Talbot, M (1994) 'Learning journals for evaluation of group-based learning', in Thorley, L and Gregory, R (eds) *Using Group-based Learning in Higher Education*, London: Kogan Page, pp.105–11.
Discusses how learning journals can help evaluate students' development of capability skills through participation in group or team work.

Chapter 4

Disciplinary Approaches and Issues in Researching Teaching

Introduction

In this chapter we look at the challenge to traditional conceptions of subjects and disciplines posed by vocationalization of the curriculum, as an area for research. We begin by examining the consequences of vocationalism for our sense of professional identity. We go on to examine two innovations which can be seen as exemplifying vocational values: the introduction of resource-based learning and the innovative use of information technology, as a means both of delivering the curriculum and of assessing it.

Background

The curriculum in higher and further education is constantly under pressure by the British government to become more vocational. Indeed the Department for Education has recently become the Department for Education and Employment, reflecting this trend. This vocationalization of the curriculum can be seen most obviously in the introduction of National Vocational Qualifications (NVQs) and General National Vocational Qualifications (GNVQs) in the post-16 curriculum. In higher education, the pressure to introduce curricula which are claimed to be more relevant to the needs of employers has taken the form of generously funded projects. The Enterprise in Higher Education Initiative, in 1987, was one attempt among others (see, for example, Atkins *et al.*, 1993) to 'seed corn' change in teaching and assessment practices to encourage active and independent learning, mainly by introducing skill elements.

Among the skills required by industry are those of team work, communication, problem solving and information technology. It is further claimed that these are transferable: skills learnt in higher education will have application in work contexts. This claim has been disputed and is a matter of current controversy. However, the underlying ideal seems unexceptionable: that students ought to be equipped to face an uncertain future in the labour market. The Employment Department's publication, *The Skills Link* (1990, cited in Atkins *et al.*, 1993) puts forward the view that higher education should be more relevant, flexible and responsive to the changing demands of the labour market; that it should take account of changes in the student body allowing for greater autonomy in learning; and exercise greater precision in the statement and assessment of learning outcomes.

Professional Identity and Definitions of Subjects

In contrast to this view of higher and further education as being flexible and portable, enabling lifelong learning, is a view of subject disciplines as being essentially about bodies of knowledge and forms of thought and enquiry into which students are initiated by lecturers whose concerns are those integral to their discipline or field of study rather than the concerns of employers. The skills connected with acquiring this body of knowledge and the associated forms of thought are not *prima facie* those represented as industry's needs. An obvious example, from the humanities, is the close reading of texts and the production of cogent arguments. It may be that this method of learning, which involves assembling information and ideas, synthesizing them, and presenting them in the form of extended prose, is displaced. An interesting question is whether new methods of teaching and assessing can be introduced without compromising the skills and attitudes thought to be necessary for the initiation of students into disciplines. A prior question, of course, relates to which skills and attitudes, body of knowledge and forms of enquiry define a discipline. Subject boundaries and definitions are frequently contested. The struggles over the definition of subjects has been well researched at secondary school level (Ball and Goodson 1984). It seems reasonable to suppose that individual lecturers who have researched in disciplines will have a good idea of versions of their discipline (or disciplines), even if they themselves do not favour them. For example, quantitative economic historians must be familiar with the work and methods of economists and historians. This line of enquiry could be researched through using unstructured interviews with lecturers in your subject discipline or field of study:

- What are the traditional teaching methods used in your discipline?
- What educational values do they embody?
- Are definitions of subjects and standards of enquiry changing to meet the demands of new sorts of curricula, and new sorts of students (for example those who have done access courses)?

The value of using an unstructured interview is that its informal nature allows for the interviewee's point of view to be fully explored. Structured and semi-structured interviews follow the interviewer's agenda and may unintentionally shut off interesting points of view (Robson, 1993).

RESEARCH TASK. UNSTRUCTURED INTERVIEW

Take a situation which is problematic for you or your colleagues. For example, it may be that you are experiencing difficulty in teaching an introductory Spanish course to students who have widely different experiences of Spanish and different levels of confidence. This could be your general area of interest and concern which you may wish to explore with other lecturers contributing to the course. You will be interested in finding out what aspects of the situation they find difficult, if any; whether they regard these aspects as important; and what effects the situation has on them, their students and their definition of their subject.

This method has the appearance of a conversation and tends therefore to be harder to analyse because its direction is unpredictable. However, it may ultimately yield more insight because categories have not been predetermined as in other forms of interview. It is important that the interviewee does most of the talking. Interviews should be transcribed and analysed. A good introduction to content analysis is to be found in Robson (1993).

Resource-based Learning

One of the consequences of introducing resource-based learning, however defined (see Gibbs and Parsons, 1994), is that students are given less face-to-face contact with a lecturer. It has been noted that, from the students' point of view, there may be a greater sense of anonymity and a sense of being unsupported. The social and emotional aspects of learning are undervalued, or at least uncatered for in courses where students are expected to exhibit a high degree of autonomy and initiative. These drawbacks may to some extent be mitigated by forms of collaborative learning where students may be required to work together on a research project. However, collaborative learning is also something that has to be learnt. It is often introduced as unproblematic. In our experience, asking students to work in groups generates as many problems as the move was intended to solve. The free-rider problem is just one example.

Our interest here, however, is in the consequences for students of learning a subject when the traditional pattern of lectures and seminars is replaced by other methods. Lectures have long been recognized as being unsatisfactory from the learners' point of view, since they necessarily presuppose a symmetry between the lecturer's intended meanings and the hearer's interpretation. Given the nature of the event it is very difficult to check whether this presupposition is true for all individuals in groups of over 30 people. Therefore mass lectures often seem to require a passive reception of information which may or may not make sense to the student. However, it does not necessarily follow that other methods are better, rather that the disadvantages are different and not yet well researched. It may be that one disadvantage of methods where the lecturer has (to a degree) relinquished control of the learning processes is that students have a weaker notion of what constitutes a subject discipline. It is possible that lectures (especially to smaller groups of people) and seminars serve to initiate students into the key questions and methods which shape a particular discipline. It may be that lecturing and conversing with a subject expert or practitioner are necessary to learning the distinctive form of discourse that shapes the discipline. If you have students working through learning packages, you could begin to investigate this area by using Kelly's self-characterization technique which is based on the idea of personal constructs. Kelly argues that each person makes sense of the world by developing constructs which are bipolar in nature. These are held, as tentative hypotheses, which we continually test and modify or extend in the light of experience. The method is to write about yourself, taking the role of a sympathetic friend. The account is therefore written in the third person. The aim is to elicit how people structure their worlds, how they see themselves in relation to these structures and the strategies they develop in order to handle their world (Bannister, 1981; Bannister and Fransella, 1971). Such a self-portrait can be examined for major themes, conflicts and references to the thoughts of others. In this particular case we would be interested in self-characterization with regard to academic subject or discipline.

RESEARCH TASK. SELF-CHARACTERIZATION

- Write about yourself. Opening lines might be:

  'I'm going to tell you about a lecturer I know'; or
  'Have you met Dr X? She is particularly interested in...'.

- If you prefer you could imagine that you are writing an academic reference for yourself.
- Analyse your own self-portrait. Try to work out how you construe your subject. Does your construct reflect employers' values?
- Using any categories that emerge, design a semi-structured interview schedule and interview a group of your students.

Reasons to Use IT

One possible response to the current challenges of increasing student group sizes, wider student diversity and decreasing contact time between lecturers and students is to develop more uses of IT and other educational technology to augment or completely take the place of some input from lecturers. However, we should also consider the equally important question of which, if any, IT activities could enhance teaching and learning in our courses. A fruitful area of research at the present time is the investigation of what benefits these approaches bring in reality.

It will be difficult to generalize for all subjects and so every lecturer can research the possibilities for their own subject specialism and then be in a position to take informed decisions about where IT activities would be appropriate and what the benefits might be. For more discussion of this on a theoretical level, see Waggoner (1994) who presents one example of a model for investigating disciplinary differences as they may relate to teaching with technology.

Student Diversity and Increased Group Size

Let us first consider strategies to deal with student diversity both in terms of subject background and, if you are contemplating using IT approaches, in IT skills. A starting point for research is to determine exactly what the students' previous experience is. For example, if you were considering IT background, you can try to determine what experience of IT the students have had before starting the course or component, what expertise this has given them and what their attitudes to IT might be. This will allow you to determine if there are any students who will be particularly disadvantaged by your use of IT. You will also be able to decide what introduction to IT the students require, ranging from a brief introduction to the package to be used and an opportunity to familiarize themselves with it, to a far deeper and longer course of instruction, perhaps itself based on computer-assisted learning (CAL) self-study tutorials, of which more later. There may be a requirement for a complete induction into the discipline of IT use, just as there is into the student's subject discipline. This is what is attempted in many institutions during the 'Introduction to IT' courses that new students attend. However, these courses too often can concentrate only on first-order skills of how to work particular pieces of software and hardware, rather than progressing to a discussion of what intellectual skills are required for really effective use. This deeper discussion might be on how to use a database effectively to go beyond the mere collection of information to the interpretation of the information and construction of meaning from it, or what is required to use a word-processor successfully to carry out the writing process in all its stages. It is an open question that you could consider as to whether such discussion can take place in a context-free environment developing transferable skills for all students, or whether each subject has its own requirements and priorities and students should be inducted into their own discipline's use of IT.

RESEARCH TASK. STUDENT AUDIT, 5-POINT SCALES

Finding out what students bring to a course can be carried out in many ways. One approach is to ask students to rate themselves on a 5-point scale with reference to a range of given statements, for example:

Rate your competence at the following activities on a scale from 1, meaning 'I am unable to carry out the activity' to 5, meaning 'I am an expert at the activity'.

- I can use a word-processor to draft text.
- I can use a computer to capture experimental data.

Indicate the extent of your agreement with the following statements on a scale from 1, meaning 'I totally agree' to 5, meaning 'I totally disagree':

- I have a positive attitude to computers.
- Computers are overrated as a means of teaching people.

For more information about this technique, see Henerson et al. (1978).

This technique also allows you to compare the changes in responses over time between two surveys. You could repeat the survey at the end of the course and attempt to draw some conclusions from the results in terms of development of skills and changes in attitude to IT, to determine the success or otherwise of the activities from an IT point of view. If you are comparing two surveys, you can either carry out a simple analysis to see which trends are apparent, or carry out more sophisticated statistical analysis to determine the significance of any perceived trends.

This approach can also be used to survey the students at the start of the course in an attempt to discover their individual learning styles. A note of caution must be sounded as students can not be neatly categorized as having a particular learning style at all times and in all situations; however, the generalization does have some value. The ideas of learning styles are discussed from an educational psychology point of view in Entwistle (1981) and one of the best known questionnaires used to examine different approaches to studying was designed by Entwistle and his colleagues at Lancaster in the UK.

Such information could be used when investigating the benefits of a particular style of IT use or a particular piece of IT courseware. You could observe how the IT was used by the students and evaluate whether different learning styles correlated with different patterns of use and hence whether particular learning styles constrained the educational effectiveness of particular IT courseware. You could also investigate whether a particular piece of IT courseware encouraged or discouraged particular styles of learning. Such a project is described in de Jong (1994) where the inventory of learning styles (ILS) diagnostic instrument is used (Vermunt, 1990). (The ILS is a collection of 120 statements which students score on a 5-point scale as in our research task. The responses allow students to be categorized as having one of four learning styles.) The students in de Jong's project worked on a piece of hypermedia-based courseware. Hypermedia is a generic term for computer-based material that allows non-linear arrangements of text, pictures and sound (for more information see Barker, 1993). In this instance a very rich multimedia environment was created, including video clips of acted scenes, information in databases, copies of articles and audio clips. The program enabled the students to investigate, reflect, make judgements and argue cases. Quantitative analysis was then carried out on measurable items such as the frequency of use of particular parts of the program and time spent on particular activities. Statistical techniques were employed to discover if there was any correlation between pattern of use and learning style. Qualitative analysis could also have been carried out on the answers the students formulated and the reasoning exhibited in the judgements given, although this is not reported in the article. From all this information the conclusions that were drawn were that although it might be thought that such a rich constructivist learning environment would lead to deeper approaches to learning, in fact this was not the case, and it appeared that the students did indeed require some form of induction into the IT discipline before they could make best use of such environments.

To continue the theme of how to cope with increased student diversity, let us now consider how the use of IT can help in the area of subject background. There has always been some diversity of ability in any student group but perhaps the range is getting wider, and you may also have to contend with a greater range of prior knowledge and experience in the subject area itself. It is suggested that self-study CAL tutorials can be a help here. These can deal with subject knowledge that is a prerequisite for a course, or basic knowledge covered during a course. The claims made for them include that they can:

- be used at a student's own pace;
- be used as often as the student wants and so concentrate on an individual's weak areas;
- be used when the student wants, free of timetable constraints;
- provide immediate feedback to the student's responses to questions and interactions.

The question that could be asked is whether the formats available begin to constrain the content considered. A possible area of research would be to consider a particular course and decide what prerequisite knowledge is required of students, what misconceptions they often have or what basic knowledge might be delivered during the course. You could then view examples of a range of types of CAL tutorial and try to see how your information might be organized in these ways.

If this approach seems fruitful the next question that arises concerns how you are going to produce the IT materials. Many packages exist that allow you to author your own materials but as with any other learning resource this requires a variety of skills, including some knowledge of learning theories. Merrill (1985) discusses the types of features authoring systems should have and considers the advantages and disadvantages of their use. It may be that the easier way out is to use an externally produced tutorial (such as are being produced in the UK for many subject areas by university consortia in the Teaching and Learning through Technology Programme), but then you must submit to constraints on content and learning approaches. It will be as if you were adopting completely the approach of a single textbook. Of course this may not be a problem if you are considering only simple prerequisites for a standard course on which there is a general consensus about content and approach.

If you did pursue this idea, an area to investigate would be how effective the tutorials were, whether they delivered what was claimed and what student attitudes were to using them. In particular you might consider if there was any feeling of alienation or loneliness engendered amongst the students from these essentially solitary activities.

The self-study tutorial approach can also be used to ameliorate the problems of increased group size. Rather than repeating basic material in a large number of tutorials this could be covered by the students individually. The approach could also help with the problems of decreased contact time: if the basics are dealt with by CAL tutorials, then the face-to-face sessions can be left free to deal with the more significant or more difficult topics. An area for research here would be to see if the claims made for time saving were true. You could monitor the time spent organizing the materials and dealing with the residue of student problems that still required face-to-face attention, and compare this to the time saved by not having to deliver the material personally. Of course it is also claimed that once CAL material is produced it can be used again and again, so some time may be saved there, but most CAL applications require an element of up-dating and other maintenance such as revision of support materials, so this should be taken into account as well. In time, if the content becomes too dated, the package may require complete redevelopment.

Enhancing Student Learning through IT Use

The kind of activities that we have been discussing so far are essentially about imparting information and checking recall and understanding. To take the discussion further into the realms of investigating the benefits of IT for enhancing learning, we must introduce some ideas from learning theory.

First, in a study by Saljo (1979), interviews were conducted with students about what they understood by learning. He was able to identify five conceptions of what learning consists of:

1. increasing knowledge;
2. memorizing information for reproduction;

3. acquiring facts, skills and procedures for later use;
4. making sense of or abstracting meaning from a situation;
5. interpreting and understanding reality.

These categories incorporate an element of development, as the first three imply a less complex view than the last two.

Second, there is a body of research (see Ramsden, 1992, for an overview) that leads to a characterization of approaches to learning as either deep or surface. Some of the defining features of the two approaches in the context of academic learning can be summarized as follows (taken from Ramsden, 1992, p.46):

Deep approach
Intention to understand. Student maintains structure of task.
Focus on 'what is signified' (eg, the author's argument, or the
    concepts applicable to solving the problem).
Relate previous knowledge to new knowledge.
Relate knowledge from different course.
Relate theoretical ideas to everyday experience.
Relate and distinguish evidence and argument.
Organize and structure content into a coherent whole.
Internal emphasis.

Surface approach
Intention only to complete task requirements. Student distorts structure of task.
Focus on the 'signs' (eg, the words and sentences of the text, or
    unthinkingly on the formula needed to solve the problem).
Focus on unrelated parts of the task.
Memorize information for assessments.
Associate facts and concepts unreflectively.
Fail to distinguish principles from examples.
Treat the task as an external imposition.
External emphasis: demands of assessments, knowledge cut off from
    everyday reality.

We can now consider particular pieces of IT courseware and attempt to evaluate them and their use in the light of these findings. While the research shows that this categorization of approaches as either deep or surface is valid for most subjects, Ramsden (1992) discusses how what constitutes these approaches can vary according to academic discipline or task within that discipline. Many specific examples of the sorts of differences found in different disciplines are contained in Entwistle and Ramsden (1983). Thus before you can start to think in terms of these approaches you need to see what these general ideas mean in relation to your own subject so that you can identify the approaches when you encounter them. When you have done this you can then attempt to develop an evaluation tool for a piece of IT courseware for use in your own subject.

RESEARCH TASK. DEVELOPING AN EVALUATION TOOL FOR IT PACKAGES

Decide on a number of headings under which you will consider the material. Then develop a general list of questions under each heading. Some items will be more important than others for a given piece of courseware, but always using the same general tool will allow you an element of comparability between material. Here are some ideas you might build on:

Content

- Does it cover the topics you require?
- Are the topics discussed at an appropriate level for the group you are intending to use it with?

Usability

- Is there a clarity of design that makes it easy for the user to see what to do at any stage?
- Is there ease of movement within the program?

Pedagogy

- Does it have clear objectives?
- Does it encourage deep or surface approaches to the learning in terms of activities you have identified for your subject?
- In terms of which of Saljo's conceptions of learning is it attempting to work, ie, is it purely offering information to be learnt or revised (category 1 or 2) or is it delivering concepts for experience and practice (category 3 or 4)?

Assessment and feedback

- What does this consist of?
- Is it assessing what you require or only what it can measure (often assessment is of quantity of activity not quality)?
- Does it feedback in a form that is useful to the lecturer, or to the student?

As well as this abstract evaluation you could also evaluate the effectiveness of the software in use. For this you could employ any of the usual approaches, eg, direct and indirect observation, questionnaires, structured and semi-structured interviews, pre- and post-tests of students, but you could also make use of information from automatic monitoring of the activity which is available only when IT is in use. This might include such information as a computer navigation trace of how a given student used the package, records of responses to interactions, answers to questions (both for a single student and for a student group), test scores, etc.

It might be worthwhile, having carried out evaluations of some particular IT packages, to consider the evaluation of generic types of courseware or approaches. Laurillard (1993) develops a general methodology for evaluating and comparing the various teaching methods and media involved in the use of educational technology. She suggests that no single approach can really address the entire learning process:

> Stand-alone media-based packages will never be sufficient, because
> none of the media can adequately support the discursive activities that
> are essential for academic learning (Laurillard, 1993, p.176).

Thus for other than the most basic uses, IT applications should be viewed as part of a package of activities in a course.

You might also think in terms of a before-during-after the activity continuum, ie, how the students must be prepared before the activity, what they should be doing during it, and how you want to use and build on what will have taken place. This will help you to evaluate the IT activity and identify the strengths and weaknesses of the approach and then decide how to augment it to enable the other learning outcomes you desire to take place.

We have already considered the generalized audit of students' IT skills and ways of ensuring they are all at approximately the same level to benefit from the proposed IT activities. Now let us consider how you might develop this before-during-after continuum for a particular activity. First, consider the 'before' phase. You could decide what the students need to know beforehand in terms of subject content, and decide on mechanisms for them to acquire this knowledge, for example other IT material, handouts, briefing sheets, prior teaching. You then can review the IT activity in operational terms and decide what the students need to carry out the activity for example, a student's guide, prompt sheets, a chance to familiarize themselves with the package. Next, consider the 'during' phase. Decide whether it is a single person or group task. Discussion between students while carrying out an activity might be a useful way of overcoming some of the deficiencies of the activity that you have identified and it may also help with alienation problems. Make clear to yourself what the learning objectives are. Decide what activities are to be carried out or tasks completed and what recording you want to take place. Finally, consider the 'after' phase. If the IT work introduced skills and procedures you could plan some activities to develop them. You may decide that the activity is deficient in the category 4 and 5 learning activities. These characteristically require reflection and evaluation on the part of the students. Discussion between the lecturer and the students would play a very important part in these stages and would need to be planned for.

Using IT in Assessment

The area of assessment was touched on in the discussion of evaluation of IT activities, but only in the context of assessment offered by a piece of software in terms of a record of how it was itself used. We can also consider the uses of IT as a tool for assessment and IT as a means of assessment. By this we mean the possibilities of the innovative use of IT materials as a vehicle for assessment. The lecturer still has to evaluate the students' work but the work will be in a non-traditional form. A suitable topic for research here would be to consider what variety of skills which we might wish students to acquire can be assessed in one IT product. For example, a group of students could produce a video presenting their findings from some project. The assessment might then include subject content, organizational skills, communication skills and ability to work as a team. Another possibility would be the production of a piece of CAL courseware using hypermedia to present an area that has been researched – something akin to an essay. Again the assessment might include subject content, clarity of design and quality of presentation. A final idea might be contributions to an e-mail conference rather than a traditional seminar. It would be hoped that the student contributions would be more considered and better researched, and perhaps more students would contribute to this forum than just the few who might dominate a face-to-face discussion.

> Part of the point of new teaching methods is that they change the nature of learning, and of what students are able to do. It follows that the teachers then have the task of rethinking the assessment of what they do (Laurillard, 1993, p.218).

The use of IT to carry out some assessment brings us back to one of our starting points: the problems of increased group size. Assessment can take up as much staff time as teaching (Gibbs and Jenkins, 1992). It is claimed that the use of IT to assess factual material or application of procedures can free lecturers from setting or marking these tests. Students will not need the lecturer to mark them or to obtain relevant feedback. This will free the lecturer to target assessment on higher level activities.

RESEARCH TASK. EVALUATION EXERCISE FOCUSING ON OBJECTIVES

Create an IT-based test for assessing a particular topic. Either this can be done from scratch using an authoring package such as Question Mark Designer, or you could adapt an existing piece of courseware. Evaluate its use in terms of:

- how much time was spent setting up the test in comparison to a traditional test;
- how much time was saved marking;
- whether the use of IT constrained the content it was possible to test;
- whether the use of IT constrained the learning outcomes it was possible to test for;
- how effective it was for the students;
- whether the IT format of the test was more stressful for the students than a traditional one (there are standard tests which determine anxiety levels connected to an event, for example the state-trait anxiety inventory; see Spielberger et al., 1970).

Development of IT materials

Having developed your evaluation skills you might now consider as a research activity the development of your own IT materials. As we have said, the existence of modern authoring packages makes the production of CAL applications very easy. However, after your experience of evaluating some of the existing packages you may feel that many of them are poorly designed and without a very clear understanding of learning theory or how to achieve their objectives. One bad example would be when a book is put into a CAL format which does not utilize the possibilities and restricts the user to a purely linear mode for development. Another would be when a completely free-form hypermedia approach is taken with no instructional design or navigation pathways to ensure the user progresses in a sensible way, and which completely loses the author's intended development of ideas or arguments.

There are a range of books and articles which deal with the development of IT material in the context of learning theories and teaching style which would start you on the right path. Some texts are recommended in the reading list below.

There are also many books and articles which consider the area of instructional design, for example Wager and Gagné (1988), Shuell (1993), and Gagné (1977) which was first published in 1965 and was the precursor to all that followed. Finally, for more detail of types of CAL materials and approaches, and a discussion of the advantages and disadvantages of each type, see Higgins *et al.* (1996).

Summary

In this chapter, we discussed how the introduction of resource-based learning and the use of IT in response to changing perceptions of our role (and to the vocationalization of the curriculum) affects our sense of professional identity and our understanding of the subjects we teach. In Chapter 5, we explore institutional and interpersonal aspects involved in the introduction of some of the innovative teaching-learning strategies we have identified and discussed in this book. Change often encounters resistance; certainly, we may have to persuade others to support our ideas, or to change their ways of thinking and of teaching. We explore the need to exercise interpersonal skills in pursuing our objectives.

Annotated Reading List

de Corte, E (1990) 'Learning with new information technologies in schools: perspectives from the psychology of learning and instruction', *Journal of Computer Assisted Learning*, 6, 69–87.
This paper argues that IT must be embedded in powerful learning environments and contains a comprehensive review of research on the three major components of a theory of learning from instruction.

Hartley, JR (1978) 'An appraisal of computer assisted learning in the UK', *Programmed Learning and Educational Technology*, 15, 2, 136–51.
This has details of research on teaching and learning with computers within the framework of a general classification scheme for teaching styles.

Laurillard, D (1993) *Rethinking University Teaching: A framework for the effective use of educational technology*, London: Routledge.
A very comprehensive book which develops a practical methodology for the design, development and implementation of educational technologies and compares and evaluates the current media and teaching methods.

O'Shea, T and Self, J (1983) *Learning and Teaching with Computers*, Brighton: Harvester.
This includes an account of the development of computer-based learning

Scrimshaw, P (ed.) (1993) *Language, Classrooms and Computers*, London: Routledge.
This is a useful collection of articles about IT in the context of learning theories and is not only about language uses.

References

Atkins, MJ, Beattie, J and Dockrell, WB (1993) *Assessment Issues in Higher Education*, report commissioned by the Employment Department, Further and Higher Education Branch.

Ball, S and Goodson, IF (1984) 'Introduction', in Goodson, IF and Ball, S (eds) *Defining the Curriculum: Histories and ethnographies*, London: Falmer Press.

Bannister, D (1981) 'Personal construct theory and research method', in Reason, P and Rowan, J (eds) *Human Inquiry: A sourcebook of new paradigm research*, Chichester: Wiley.

Bannister, D and Fransella, F (1971) *Inquiring Man*, Harmondsworth: Penguin.

Barker, P (1993) *Exploring Hypermedia*, London: Kogan Page.

de Jong, FPCM (1994) 'A constructivist technology-enriched learning environment and the claim on students' self-regulation', in Gibbs, G (ed.) *Improving Student Learning: Theory and practice*, Oxford: Oxford Centre for Staff Development, Oxford Brookes University.

Entwistle, NJ (1981) *Styles of Learning and Teaching: An integrated outline of educational psychology*, Chichester: Wiley.

Entwistle, NJ and Ramsden, P (1983) *Understanding Student Learning*, Beckenham: Croom Helm.

Gagné, RM (1977) *The Conditions of Learning*, New York: Holt, Rhinehart and Winston.

Gibbs, G and Jenkins, A (eds) (1992) *Teaching Large Classes in Higher Education*, London: Kogan Page.

Gibbs, G and Parsons, C (eds) (1994) *Course Design for Resource-based Learning Education*, Oxford: The Oxford Centre for Staff Development, Oxford Brookes University.

Henerson, ME, Morris, LL and Fitz-Gibbon, CT (1978) *How to Measure Attitudes*, London: Sage.

Higgins, C, Reading, J and Taylor, P (1996) *Researching into Learning Resources in Colleges and Universities*, London: Kogan Page.

Laurillard, D. (1993) *Rethinking University Teaching: A framework for the effective use of educational technology*, London: Routledge.

Merrill, D (1985) 'Where is the author in authoring?', *Journal of Computer Based Instruction*, 12, 4, 90–96.

O'Shea, T and Self, J (1983) *Learning and Teaching with Computers*, Brighton: Harvester.

Ramsden, P (1992) *Learning to Teach in Higher Education*, London: Routledge.

Robson, C (1993) *Real World Research: A resource for social scientists and practitioner researchers*, Oxford: Blackwell.

Saljo, R (1979) 'Learning in the learner's perspective: Some common sense conceptions', Reports from the Institute of Education 76, University of Gothenberg.

Shuell, T (1993) 'Designing instructional computing systems for meaningful learning', in Jones, M and Winne, P (eds) *Adaptive Learning Environments: Foundations and frontiers*, Berlin: Springer-Verlag.

Spielberger, CD, Gorsuch, RL and Lushene, RE (1970) *Test Manual for the State-Trait Anxiety Inventory*, Palo Alto, CA: Consulting Psychologists Press.

Vermunt, JDHM (1990) *Skilful Studying of Social Sciences. Part 2: Guide for students*, Tilburg, Germany: Tilburg University.

Wager, W and Gagné, RM (1988) 'Designing computer aided instruction', in Jonassen, D (ed.) *Instructional Designs for Microcomputer Courseware*, London: Lawrence Erlbaum Associates.

Waggoner, MD (1994) 'Disciplinary differences and the integration of technology into teaching', *Journal of Information Technology for Teacher Education*, 3, 2, 175–86.

Chapter 5

Researching Institutional and Interpersonal Aspects of Innovative Teaching and Learning

It has already been suggested in this book that tutors in higher education may not be as autonomous as they are sometimes thought to be, both with respect to what they teach and to how they teach. Just as subject-based cultures influence teaching methods, so do institutional cultures (see Chapter 4 for a discussion of subject cultures). In this chapter, we begin by exploring some institutional factors which influence what and how we teach, then discuss interpersonal factors which, arguably, are involved in almost everything we do as professional educators. For example, if we are initially mentored by a senior colleague, or are appointed to an institution in which courses are commonly co-taught, we will not have an absolute say in designing or delivering our courses. Without exercising interpersonal skills, we will be unable to bring about change. Mentors will have their own way of delivering and organizing their courses, and it will be difficult for us, as a novice, to suggest changes. Our mentor may feel threatened, or think they are wasting their time with a colleague who obviously thinks that they have nothing to learn from their experience. If we are a member of a course team, an existing approach to delivery may dominate at the expense of our new ideas. Such institutional factors as large size groups, small size groups, a low or high tutor-student ratio will all, as discussed elsewhere in this book, also affect our freedom to deliver courses as we want to, and will tend to dictate what is pedagogically possible, or impossible. In fact, lecturers and tutors are at the centre of a 'web of forces that act upon' them, 'some more strongly than others, but all influencing... professional behaviour' (Musgrave, 1972, p.160). First, we shall discuss the somewhat arcane question, 'Do institutions think?' and suggest some appropriate research tasks, then explore interpersonal factors which affect our autonomy as lecturers and tutors.

Do Institutions Think?

The answer, in one sense, is obviously 'No'. Institutions do not think because they are not alive, and do not possess brains. However, in another sense, and here enters the arcane, they do 'think'. There is often talk about institutions 'refusing to die', as if, despite what we have just said, they are actually alive. We also talk about institutional ethos, or culture, as if these somehow stem from the institutions themselves, independently of the people who work in (or who inhabit) the institution. We have probably all experienced what is meant by an institutional culture, and something of how it influences our own thinking. For example, if we join a conservative club (this might be any type of club, say a London gentlemen's club), we will expect the culture to reflect this ethos. We will feel it appropriate to think conservatively ourselves. Should we become aware of a liberal idea forming in our minds, we will probably suppress this, either because it seems inappropriate, a betrayal of what the institution stands for, or because colleagues will disapprove. We revisit the metaphor of 'club culture' later in this chapter.

Anthropologist Mary Douglas has explored some of these issues in her book, *How Institutions Think* (1987). She acknowledges the influence of Emile Durkheim (1858–1917), who was professor of sociology and education at the Sorbonne, and is perhaps most famous for his consensus theory of how societies function. Durkheim believed that societies, social systems and institutions function because their members agree on fundamental codes of conduct and values, and on parameters of acceptable and unacceptable behaviour. Once this consensus has emerged, societies and institutions produce their own signs and symbols (we can call these 'cultures') which help to perpetuate their ethos, or belief systems. He coined the term 'conscience collective' to describe this phenomenon, 'the set of beliefs and sentiments common to the average member of a single society that has its own life' (cited in Seymour-Smith, 1986, p.52). Durkheim saw punishment as one way in which society enforces or polices its code; in fact, by reinforcing the social conventions, crime – according to Durkheim – may actually perform a beneficial function. Change, for Durkheim, is therefore problematic: if individuals challenge the accepted codes, they do so in opposition to the 'conscience collective' to which they have themselves delegated responsibility for ensuring social cohesion.

Applying Durkheimian theory to small-scale institutions, Douglas (1987) explores the extent to which different kinds of institutions allow individuals to think different kinds of thoughts and to respond to different emotions. One important aspect is the extent to which individuals are prepared to sink their private interests for a common good, or to silence their own ideas if these are opposed to dominant ones. 'Any institution', she suggests, can also 'control the memory of its members', causing 'them to forget experiences incompatible with its righteous image' and brings 'to their minds events which sustain the view of nature which is complimentary to itself'. They 'provide categories of thought', set 'the terms for self-knowledge', and 'fix identities' (p.112).

Applying this to teaching methods, it follows that an institution where the traditional lecture dominates, or where staff are not trained in small-group techniques, might well resist the introduction of a teaching strategy such as student-led team work. Similarly, an institution which regards lecturers as subject experts might resist the introduction of peer assessment. If we want to introduce learning contracts, for example, we may discover that our 'institutional system... is culturally at odds with that implied by the use of learning contracts' (Stephenson and Laycock, 1993, p.162). Innovation of any type is often, if not always, regarded as a challenge to the existing culture which will have an in-bred tendency to transmit and to preserve itself. This is what is meant by the oft-heard phrase, 'institutional momentum'. Incidentally, by 'institution', Douglas means 'customs' as well as social organizations (for example, a graduation ceremony or a formal college meal). Whichever culture we join, we are likely to find ourselves adopting attitudes and practices (teaching methods) which are part of the 'way things are' within that culture. Yet changes do occur and can be made to happen. To promote change, we need to know what type of organizational culture our institution has so that we can operate effectively within it.

Four Different Types of Organizational Culture

Handy (1988) has usefully identified four different types of organizational culture. Each type, he suggests, involves a different dynamic between individual staff, and their relationship with the institution. Handy emphasizes that:

> there are no wholly good cultures and no wholly bad cultures. All cultures are OK (sic), in the right place, because each culture is good for some things, less good for others (p.109).

Club Cultures

The first type is the 'club culture'. This, as Handy describes it, resembles our example of the conservative club used earlier. People are attracted to work in an institution which has a club culture because they share its ideals and goals and like its way of working. In other words, clubs attract like-minded people (or those who are prepared to restrain their individuality in order to conform to the accepted pattern). Club members often look alike, perhaps wearing a club tie, or blazer, or conforming to particular dress codes. Change in a club culture happens when a consensus emerges amongst members, rather than when one individual takes the initiative. Consultation, amongst the like-minded, says Handy, is probably informal and proceeds in a 'personal, telepathic, empathetic style' (p.109). Club cultures, though, are not usually very conscious of rank, and thus consultation moves horizontally rather than vertically. This resembles what Ball (1987), who identifies three different types of organizations, calls a 'membership controlled' organization.

Role Cultures

The next type of organizational culture identified by Handy is the 'role' model:

> The best picture is the kind of organisation chart that all these organisations have. It looks like a pyramid of boxes, inside each box is a job title with an individual's name in smaller type below, indicating who is currently the occupant of that box, but of course the box continues even if the individual departs (p.110).

These cultures tend to expect individuals to fulfil their prescribed roles, as specified, much as the previous occupant of the box did, rather than to work out their own styles of operating. Each successive occupant of a role is a clone of their predecessor. The route for proposing change would be a formal one – and any proposal would move upwards, through the hierarchy, in a vertical rather than horizontal direction. Role cultures may resist innovation if it involves major changes in the neatly laid out organization chart! This resembles Ball's 'hierarchical organization'. Memoranda, says Handy, will tend to go formally from 'job title' to 'job title', rather than from 'first name' to 'first name'.

Task Cultures

The third type of organizational culture is the 'task culture'. This, says Handy, is the preferred culture of many competent people, because they work in groups, sharing both skills and responsibilities; they are constantly working on new challenges since every task is different (p.111).

Roles remain, but tasks come and go; thus:

> Task cultures... tend to be full of young, energetic people developing and testing talents: people who are self-confident enough not to worry about long-term security – at least until they are a bit older (p.111).

Overt hierarchy is minimal and roles are much less rigidly prescribed than they are in a role culture. The stress is on getting jobs done, rather than on who does them or on how they are done. In other words, there is no built-in tendency towards doing jobs in a particular, traditional way. New, different, creative ways of doing them are encouraged rather than discouraged. This flexible approach means that change and innovation are part of the norm, rather than exceptions. This resembles Ball's 'professional organization'. Professional people are expected to be competent in their own areas of expertise, capable of independent thought as well as of performing routine tasks. Indeed, it is often assumed that creativity is part of many professions – architecture and advertising, for example.

People Cultures

Finally, there is the 'people culture'. The other types,

> put the organisation first and then, in their different ways, harness the individual to this purpose. The person culture puts the individual first and makes the organisation the resource for the individual's talents (p.112).

In educational institutions, with the increased emphasis on attracting external funds, the type of research centres which build up around a single individual qualify as examples of people cultures. Research grants and assistants are primarily used to serve the purposes of the individual who has attracted the funding. Controlled by individuals, people cultures are by definition hierarchical, although they do not always operate as such, depending very much on the personality and life-style preference of the central individual. They may gather around themselves people who, while competent, are unlikely to challenge their own central role. Or, they may gather around themselves a team of creative and risk-taking individuals.

Most large institutions will be more complex and diverse than these models suggest. They will contain examples of all four as well as various combinations of them. For example, one department may be a club culture, consisting of like-minded people, another may be a people culture, perhaps the finance department is a role culture, while the department for extramural or extension studies, or for professional development, is a task culture. There may be official mechanisms in place for sanctioning major developments or changes in practice; there may be parallel, unofficial channels, which must also be pursued if any formal proposal is to succeed. Most institutions comprise a series of inter-connecting 'micro-political cultures' within what we might think of as a 'macro-political system'. The task of the manager, says Handy, is to 'gather the cultural forces together, using the strengths of each in the right places. It is not an easy task...' (p.116).

The micro-political cultures with which we may have to deal will include 'private' as well as 'public' ones (that is, informal networks as well as official committee processes). As Hoyle (1989) says:

> Micropolitics can be said to consist of the strategies by which
> individuals and groups in organisational contexts seek to use their
> resources of authority and influence to further their interests (p.66).

Introducing Change

Many of the teaching methods discussed in this book can be introduced by individual teachers, within their own courses, without the need to gain official sanction or approval. This is especially true if there are no major cost implications. Other innovations, however, will require some form of official sanction. How we pursue this will vary according to the particular organizational culture, or cultures, within which we have to operate. If one's own department is a club culture, the way to introduce change would be to discuss informally with colleagues until a general consensus in favour of your proposal emerges. Usually, by the time it is introduced it will have been owned by the whole culture (or 'member-ship'), and your own role in initiating the innovation is likely to be forgotten. This is because club cultures operate best when everyone involved thinks that they had the same idea all along! If we operate in a person culture, the best strategy may well be to convince the person around whom the culture revolves that the idea is theirs. Innovations, such as the production of resource-based learning materials, have obvious cost implications and will certainly require official sanction. This will probably involve dealing with the role culture mentality which does not especially like entrepreneurial ideas. If we want to pursue major initiatives, we will need to know how to operate as effective agents of change within our organization's culture or cultures.

Before attempting to introduce a major proposal, a preliminary exercise would be to map out the official and unofficial channels we will need to pursue. If we can identify which organizational cultures are involved, we will also be able to identify whether we will need to persuade groups, individuals, or complex combinations of these! If we are aware of a major innovation within our institution, or within a particular department, we could usefully – to borrow a phrase from systems analyses – conduct an 'audit trail', asking who began the initiative. Was it an individual, or a group? How did they consult others? Which committees were formally consulted? Did key people in the hierarchy lend support, or oppose the idea? What lessons can we learn from this? By reconstructing an 'audit trail' we will then be able to draw a chart of our institution, indicating the different types of organizational culture involved in the process.

The following schema, suggested by Earley and Fletcher-Campbell (1992) may be of use in charting how decisions are made within your institution. This schema locates management styles along a left–right spectrum. Those towards the left leave no, or little room for participation in the decision-making process by subordinates; those towards the right allow for consultation, or delegate decision-making to subordinates. For example, on the left, the manager 'makes decisions and announces them'; towards the middle, the manager 'presents ideas and invites suggestions', towards the right, the manager 'defines limits, asks groups to make decision' (see p.183). Ashcroft, Jones and Siraj-Blatchford (forthcoming), writing about the aims and ethics of further education, also explore how different people within the same institution may have different perspectives, and suggest some relevant research task. (For example, are there differences between the aims of an institution, and the perceived implementation of its aims? See Chapter 2.)

Below, we suggest two research tasks which may help us explore the relationship between institutional cultures and innovation in course delivery or teaching methodology.

RESEARCH TASK. MODIFIED FOCUS GROUP TECHNIQUE (PHOTOGRAPHS)

(Based on the focus group technique method; see Ashcroft et al., 1996, ch. 2.)

This research task explores staff and student perceptions of the learning ethos within your institution, and whether it matches student/staff values. Research questions might be:

- Is there perceived to be a bias towards a particular style of course delivery at the expense of alternatives?
- Are colleagues aware of any particular pressure to use certain teaching methods as opposed to alternatives?

There is some overlap between this research task and the one we suggest below. Both will help to create a picture of the relationship, within your institution, between teacher autonomy, and the Institution itself. A version of the focused group discussion, as outlined below, might be used:

1. Invite a mixed group of staff and students to participate in a collaborative research exercise.

2. Ask participants to describe, or perhaps to represent non-verbally, their impression of the teaching-learning ethos, for example, by taking photographs around the institution which illustrate their conception of the teaching-learning ethos.

- How would they characterize it?
- How do they think the role of the tutor is perceived by the institute (eg, subject expert, expert in how others learn, etc)?
- How do they think students are perceived by the institute (as empty vessels which need to be filled up, as partners in the learning-teaching enterprise, etc)?
- Are participants aware of any change or changes in these perceptions since they first joined the institute?

If photographs have been used, ask members of the group to describe the teaching-learning ethos which they think the photographer had in mind. Next, find out if the photographer agrees or disagrees with their perceptions. Discuss differences to see if it is possible to arrive at a consensus. Do staff and students perceive the ethos differently?

3. If participants are aware of changes, are there differences between how students and staff perceive these changes? What is perceived to have driven changes – pedagogical rationale, or economic and political factors?

RESEARCH TASK. MODIFIED LIFE HISTORY METHOD
(SNAKE CHARTS)

This research task explores with colleagues how their own approach to teaching and their use of different teaching methods has evolved, and is designed to enhance lecturers' understanding of the organizational culture in which they operate. The following questions could be researched:

- To what extent has their teaching practice been influenced by senior colleagues, by institutional convention, or policy?
- Are colleagues aware of any relation between changes in their own practice and factors external to themselves as tutors and lecturers?

A modified life history research strategy (see Chapter 2 for another application of this method) might be adopted, using snake charts to plot changes in thinking about teaching, and to chart moments of particular significance in creating or stimulating change. The following could be used during a staff development day as a joint reflective exercise.

1. Ask colleagues willing to participate in a research project to chart:

- the teaching methods they use now which they did not use when they first entered the institution, and to note when they began using these methods;
- the teaching methods which they used previously but do not use now, and to note when they ceased using these teaching methods.

2. Ask participants to reflect on why they ceased to use the latter and adopted the former and to identify factors which impacted on their decision to change teaching styles, eg institutional policy, personal dissatisfaction, desire to experiment, result of student assessment, etc.

The snake chart could be used as follows: ask participants to list, in chronological order, the different teaching methods they have used, and are using, on a meandering, snake-like line down the middle of the page and to link these with any critical or significant events which stimulated or caused change, by describing these events or stimuli in the margins.

3. Chart the results of the above exercise (perhaps using another snake chart) to see if there are any common trends at any given time, for example, towards a new teaching method.

4. Survey educational publications for each period to identify whether trends you have chartered correspond with any general tendencies in educational theory and practice. Also try to see if the reasons stated for introducing change are the same, similar, or diverse. Are changes mainly attributable to personal reasons, or to institutional ones? Are educational rationales for changes developed after events have actually been driven by economic or political factors?

Interpersonal Relationships and their Effect on Teaching and Learning

Implicit in what we have already said about different organizational cultures and their implications for how we might introduce new ideas into our institutions, is the importance of interpersonal skills. Even if we are able to implement changes without involving colleagues, we will have to involve our students. Interpersonal skills are involved in any innovation within teaching and learning. If we introduce group work, peer or self-assessment, the use of resource-based learning, or any of the teaching-learning strategies mentioned in this book, we will need to convince students of the worthwhileness and advantages of what we demand of them. This may not be as easy as we think. Gosling (1993), for example, who explores using informal learning contracts to encourage students to develop seminar skills, comments:

> So far on, the evidence suggests that learning contracts encourage
> independent working and prepare students for contact with
> employers. A major difficulty is that of persuading the students that
> capability skills are as necessary as subject or content (p.69).

Obviously, too, interpersonal skills become crucial for students when engaged in many of these collaborative teaching-learning strategies.

Even when we think that we are acting completely independently of others, we may well find that our work is directly affected by what others have, or have not done. For example, while we may like to check audio-visual equipment ourselves before beginning a lecture, busy time-tables may not allow is to do so. Instead, we will need to depend on technicians ensuring that equipment works, and on other colleagues informing them when problems occur so that repairs can be made. Other factors may also affect our ability to do what we want to do in the lecture or seminar – size, or shape of the room allocated, equipment available for use, etc. The criteria used for allocating rooms may not always deliver what we require. For example, one of the authors has had rooms allocated which, while they can accommodate the number of students in the group, are the wrong shape for small group work.

Attitudes towards Teaching and Learning

In a traditional lecture, when the tutor disseminates knowledge into the atmosphere of the lecture room, each student is individually responsible for picking up this knowledge. No particular interpersonal relationship between individual students is demanded, except to refrain from making too much noise. Nor is the actual relationship between the tutor and the students very complex or demanding. It is not even necessary for the tutor to know the names of the students. For that matter, provided that they believe the tutor to be competent in the subject being studied, students do not actually need to know his or her name either! Neither knowing nor not knowing names in this context will affect the learning process. There are, of course, certain assumptions about the respective roles of tutor and student which operate within the lecture room. The tutor expects the students to listen respectfully to the lecture, to raise points of clarification (but not to engage in debate which will prevent the lecturer covering the syllabus), and to take responsibility for recording the material. In this sense, students are responsible for their own learning but they are not required to make decisions over content, or to contribute very much to this from out of their own experience. They are not required to engage very deeply with their own learning experience. Their role is, mainly, a passive one. The students expect the lecturer to disseminate to them the information they will need to pass the examination, or to tell them where and how they can access this information. Should such lectures and recommended reading not prepare them adequately for the examination, students are likely to complain that the lecturer has failed to do the job properly. In a sense, both students and tutor are here occupying 'boxes' within a role culture. Personality does not play a very significant part in either party fulfilling their expected roles nor, within the parameters of this view of the teaching-learning task, from doing so successfully.

In sharp contrast, developmental, open or deep approaches to the teaching-learning process demand the exercise of interpersonal skills between tutors and students and also between the students themselves. Demanding partnership, dialogue and negotiation, such teaching-learning strategies all draw on the related notions of the reflective tutor and the reflective student. In this model, tutors constantly reflect on how they can improve their facilitation of others' learning; students reflect on how they can take increasing responsibility for their own learning, and how they can improve their learning. Ashcroft and Foreman-Peck (1994) addressing tutors, write:

> We put forward the view that part of your role may be to facilitate your students' development as reflective practitioners of their subject. This... implies that they are willing to take responsibility for their own learning and to contribute to that of others.... It is our belief that part of your job as a tutor is to create the conditions to enable this development and ethos of study and analyses that is worthwhile for its own sake... (p.8).

We have already identified some of the skills involved in being a facilitator of learning rather than a subject expert (see Chapter 3). However, we may usefully explore this in much more detail. Here, our concern is to understand how interpersonal skills and different types of interpersonal relations may help or hinder our efforts to introduce innovation in teaching-learning methods. This discussion is intended to be of use both in implementing innovation within the lecture room and in pursuing ideas with colleagues within the wider institutional context, especially if we need to win their support or attract official sanction or approval for our proposals.

'Know Thyself'

In order to understand how other people work best, we first need to understand how we work ourselves. This understanding will be crucial in any attempt to involve others, whether colleagues or students, in new modes of working. If students who are used to being treated as empty vessels are suddenly expected to take control of the learning process, they will flounder. Similarly, if colleagues are used to being regarded, and to regarding themselves, as subject experts, are suddenly expected to be experts in how others learn, they will also flounder. To prevent this, we will need to put strategies in place which will enable those involved to fulfil their new roles. Incidentally, both practitioner and own-institution (or insider) research begin with the researcher identifying their own ideas, preconceptions and bias. We shall add a note about the need for reflexivity towards the end of this chapter.

Life-style Preferences

Friedlander (1975) has identified three different 'life-style preferences' which, we shall suggest, influence how people learn and how they might react to innovation (see Ashcroft and Foreman-Peck, 1994, p.45). These three life-style preferences are the formalistic, the sociocentric and the personalistic. There may be some correlation between these styles (or types) and the different organizational cultures in which people tend to prefer working. Each style has its strengths and weaknesses, and the ability to draw appropriately on each is an interpersonal skill well worth developing. 'Formalistic types' prefer to work in systems within which people's roles, remits and responsibilities are clearly defined. Such people would probably feel comfortable in a role culture, as described above. They may well have very clear personal goals, involving moving up through the hierarchy of boxes as each 'system' is mastered and appropriate targets are achieved efficiently. Arguably, systems people tend to neglect the personal element involved in, for example, problem-solving (that is, individuals' perceptions and experiences) favouring instead systems. Ideally, systems work regardless of the particular people who happen, at any given time, to operate them – people are regarded as parts of the mechanism, performing a function like any other part. As Ashcroft and Foreman-Peck point out, the weakness of a systems approach is its impatience with 'the ambiguities that working with people involves'. Its strength is its ability to 'work systematically and to organise a lot of information' (p.45). Systems often seem inflexible, even arbitrary, to those outside. For example, why is the size of a group, rather than what a tutor wants to do with the group, used (if it is so used) as the main criterion for allocating use of rooms? Change, though, obviously does take place within these cultures, where it is brought about by activating the relevant authorization process and by exerting one's influence within that system.

Sociocentric people, according to Freidlander, are those who work well in and with groups. However, they are perhaps also likely to over-value 'social harmony at the expense of the task in hand' (p.45). The club culture might well be their preferred setting. As we suggested towards the beginning of this chapter, members of a club tend to look alike – if you are the only one not wearing the same blazer, you will be, and feel, conspicuous. Sociocentric types tend to pull in the same direction; they like consensus and agreement. If the formalist likes to avoid any deviation from or disagreement with the established order of things, then the sociocentric type wants rather to avoid disagreement with the group. Change occurs less by activating committee mechanisms than through group discussion and participation.

In contrast, the personalistic type is willing to be the odd one out, willing to express their own ideas, even if these are unpopular. They are often very creative people, willing to take risks, sometimes even to 'consider what is right rather than what is good for their career' (p.45). Unlike the formalist, they will be impatient with a role or systems approach. Their ideal organizational culture is probably the people culture, with themselves at the centre. What they dislike most of all is being untrue to themselves, whether or not 'being true' leads to disagreement with either the established order or the immediate group. If they want to introduce change in practice, or for that matter in theory, their preferred route is to confront issues and people.

The old adage that like-attracts-like may mean that we naturally incline towards working with people who share our preference. On the other hand, the ideal working environment is probably one in which these preferences mix – some people being prepared to launch new ideas; others, more cautious, needing persuading so that in the process the idea is tested, gains support and becomes owned by the wider group or team. Obviously, few of us resemble any of the above types in all aspects, but we may very well tend towards one of them. In order to operate effectively, we should be able to draw on the strengths of each. For example, if we want to bring about change within a club culture, we will need the strengths of the sociocentric type, who works well with groups and finds it easy to create a climate of consensus. If we have to persuade systems people to support our proposal, we will need to be able to present a clear picture of organizational implications, costs and how peoples' roles will be affected, which all draw on the strengths of the formalist type. However, our focus in this book is on teaching methods and on enhancing the quality of our pedagogy, so the research tasks we suggest below will relate directly to this focus.

As suggested above, collaborative teaching-learning methods involve interpersonal skills. While our life-style preferences do influence how we work individually, when we work by ourselves they do not impact very much, if at all, on other people. As soon as we begin to work with others, in a team or group, our preferred style will affect other people's performance. We will need to develop sensitivities towards the strengths and weaknesses of other people's preferred modes of working, in order to make appropriate use of the former for the benefit of the whole group. Before introducing an innovation involving partnership, team or group work, task one below might usefully help us to identify students' life-style preferences. This will enable us to set goals for the development of interpersonal skills during the course itself. Students, too, have different orientations to learning. Some will view the process competitively: they will regard education as a competition (to score higher marks than their peers), or as competing with others for scarce resources. Others may be more sympathetic towards learning collaborative strategies. We would argue that, if we want to include capability skills as outcome objectives, these should be made explicit to students from the beginning of the course. In this view, the most important aspect of higher learning is the acquisition of higher-order thinking, rather than of information about a subject. Barnett (1992) writes:

> Higher learning calls for higher order thinking on the part of the
> student. Whether engaged in propositional thought or in professional
> action, students should be encouraged to develop the capacity to keep
> an eye on themselves, and to engage in a critical dialogue with

themselves in all they think and do. It is a higher order of thinking that is called for here, a metadiscourse; and literally a higher education, because it is a reflective process in which the student interrogates her/his thoughts and practice (p.198).

RESEARCH TASK. QUESTIONNAIRE (BI-POLAR)

Design a questionnaire to elicit information about how students interact with others. You may want to employ the three types discussed above (formalist, sociocentric and personalist) to help analyse the data, or you may prefer to invent some categories of your own. Use questions such as:

- Do you prefer to work alone, or with others?
- Do you contribute to group discussions frequently, sometimes, rarely?

These ought to elicit useful information. Other questions, such as, 'When you want clarification or extra information, do you ask for it' will help identify how proactive students are in extending their learning, or whether they have difficulty with seeking appropriate assistance from others.
   The questionnaire could be a 'bi-polar' type, for example:

I enjoy working with others: agree/disagree (circle your response).

It will also be useful to ask participants to identify interpersonal skills which they believe they contribute to group work, and those which they believe require improvement. It may be interesting to check students' self-perception against others' perception of their interpersonal skills. This could be built into a discussion or seminar at the beginning of the course about its aims and objectives, and on study skills involved in working collaboratively. Students could discuss their questionnaire responses in pairs, and comment afterwards on whether the discussion has changed how they perceive themselves. The object of this exercise is to facilitate the setting of development goals which can later be used for evaluation (at the end of the course). For advice on questionnaire design, see Ashcroft *et al.* (1996, ch. 2).

   Having identified areas for improvement, student self-development can be built into the overall outcome objectives of the course, alongside academic goals. A similar exercise, conducted at the end of the year, term, or semester, could then evaluate success or failure in meeting these objectives. As a research project, the exercise might also explore whether what, for participants, may be a new emphasis on development goals obstructs or assists the achievement of academic goals. This will also test whether the claims we make about collaborative and interactive teaching-learning methods (for example, that they encourage deep learning) are justified by the results. If they are not, we may need to rethink our rationale for using these strategies instead of, say, the traditional lecture.

RESEARCH TASK. PARTICIPANT OBSERVATION

The research task above focuses on student experience of an innovation, and seeks to assess and evaluate whether skill needs identified at the beginning of the course are developed by the course. Perhaps closely related to this is the role of the tutor in encouraging and facilitating students in the development of interpersonal skills. What strategies can the tutor adopt? The following issues might be explored:

- Which interpersonal skills do you expect students to exercise during the course?
- Which skills do you think individual students are bringing to the course, and what development needs have they (and you) identified (perhaps drawing on information from a questionnaire, together with your own observations)?
- How do you think students might improve these?
- What can you do, as tutor, to facilitate improvement?

1. Select students with a range of orientations towards group work, and note in your research diary the skills they have identified for improvement.
2. Observe how students interact with others in their groups and how they respond to any interventions from you intended to help them to develop their skills.
3. Note which strategies work and which do not. Be explicit about the criteria you are using to evaluate success and failure.

As you test ideas and strategies, record what happens and any evidence you collect which suggests their success or failure. The result of this research could be used to design an observation schedule which other tutors could use during group work to help monitor and evaluate the teaching-learning process. *Using Group-based Learning in Higher Education* (1994) edited by Thorley and Gregory might usefully be consulted before beginning these research tasks. This book gives hints about how seminars can be used to help students develop relevant skills, and on how the tutor can contribute to the skilling process. Bell (1993) describes a method for 'interaction-process analyses' which could be used to help design an observation schedule. This suggests various categories to describe interventions during group meetings, such as 'proposing' and 'disagreeing'. We might use such categories as 'links with previous intervention', or 'goes off at a tangent', or 'interrupts', and so on. These are each numbered and printed across the top of the observation sheet. Names of group members are then printed in a vertical line down the left-hand side, and the squares thus created are ticked to identify the nature of each intervention. Totalling these will also show how often each member participated in the group discussion (see Bell, pp.112–16). If a strategy is being tested to encourage a given student to contribute more often or to refrain from unhelpful intervention, such a record will be of considerable help in evaluating the usefulness of the strategy under review.

Reflexivity and Ethical Issues in Insider Research

Research within one's own institution has its advantages and disadvantages. The type of observation suggested in the research task above has its roots in ethnographic participant observer research which, traditionally, was conducted in a society, community, culture or institution other than your own. The ethnographer, having entered the institution from the outside, then attempted to gather data from as diverse a sample as possible (ensuring that male/female, young/old, leader/led, official/dissident voices were heard) before returning home to write their report. It was often assumed that the field worker was completely objective, neutral and scientific in the conduct of their research. The account rendered was thus authoritative – and if 'the natives' could not quite recognize themselves in the account this was because, as Evans-Pritchard once said, ethnographers discover 'in native society what no native can explain to him and what no layman, however conversant with the culture, can perceive – its basic structure, a set of abstractions' (cited in Lewis, 1992, p.371).

In other words, the outsider may see what insiders can not see about themselves; there is a 'taken for grantedness' about what we do. However, early ethnographic accounts, often unread by those about whom they were written, were in a sense 'created' by the researcher. We only have their word to support the genuineness of the account (and perhaps any evidence of 'triangulation' contained in the account). On the other hand, properly conducted outsider research may indeed produce an account which is broader and more detailed than the perspective of any individual informant or consultant, all of whose views will be influenced by their own particular life-style preferences, as well as by their roles and status within the institution. Arguably, it may be harder for insider researchers to construct the 'broad picture' than outsiders, since the temptation to see everything through the lens of their own perspectives may be difficult to avoid. This is a strong argument in favour of inviting researchers from outside. However, by exercising 'reflexivity', the insider researcher can overcome this problematic.

There are now few social scientists who believe that any ethnographic study can be conducted 'in some autonomous realm that is insulated from the wider society and from the particular biography of the researcher... in such a way that its findings can be unaffected by social processes and personal characteristics' (Hammersley and Atkinson, 1995, p.16). Rather, it is recognized that:

> research is an active process, in which accounts of the world are produced through selective observation and theoretical interpretation of what is seen, through asking particular questions and interpreting what is said in reply, through writing fieldnotes and transcribing audio-visual recordings, as well as through writing research reports (*ibid*, p.18).

The researcher's own interests, agenda, biases and personality all influence this process, whether they are insiders or outsiders. Thus, says Neuman (1994):

> A... researcher takes advantage of her personal insights, feelings and perceptions... but... takes measures to guard against the influence of prior beliefs or assumptions... rather than hiding behind 'objective' techniques, she is forthright and makes her values explicit in a report (p.322).... Fieldwork involves social relationships and personal feelings.... Personal, subjective experiences are part of field data... surprise, indignation or questioning... may become an opportunity for reflection and analysis (p.341).

'Reflexivity' means constantly reflecting on our feelings, on how these may be shaping or influencing our research. For example, we may passionately believe that many changes in teaching methods, or in course design and delivery in our institution have been driven by financial or pragmatic rather than by educational considerations. We may want to draw attention to what we perceive as a need for greater educational input into policy making within our institution. In commencing the research suggested above, we would need to declare this belief, and take measures during the research to guard against selecting data to confirm the conviction. Of course, our research may well do just this but it will only be taken seriously, given our declared bias, if readers are convinced that we did not in some way manipulate the research process to support our preconceived ideas.

Does Insider Research have any Particular Advantages?

As we have already suggested, outsider researchers may very well succeed in constructing an holistic picture of the system, culture, or institute they study which can help insiders to understand themselves better. However, they then return home. It is insiders who are left to implement any recommendations. These, however convincing and well intended the report, will appear to be imposed from without, as indeed they are. Insider researchers, on the other hand, remain within their institutions, and share some responsibility for implementing change. Simons (1989) has argued for a democratic approach to educational research which enables people to own the research for themselves (including its consequences). Those who participate ought to be involved not only in volunteering data, but also in recording and analysing it and in following its implications through within their own professional practice. This type of democratic, participatory research also reduces the gap, sometimes assumed, between theory and practice.

Schon (1983), who developed the notion of reflective practice, argued that it offers an alternative understanding to the traditional 'hierarchical model' of what constitutes knowledge. He wrote:

> As one would expect from the hierarchical model of professional
> knowledge, research is institutionally separate from practice,
> connected to it by carefully defined relationships of exchange.
> Researchers are supposed to provide the basic and applied science
> from which to derive techniques for diagnosing and solving the
> problems of practice. Practitioners are supposed to furnish researchers
> with problems for study and with tests of the utility of research results.
> The researcher's role is distinct from, and usually considered superior
> to, the role of the practitioner (p.26).

The type of research suggested in this chapter (and throughout this book) assumes that the researcher has a vested interest in putting their research to constructive use within their own institutional and professional contexts. Unlike outsiders, they can not walk away from the situations within which their research was conducted, nor easily hide behind the shield of anonymity. Even when tasks can be carried out without the assistance of others, our colleagues will know that we are engaged in research, and will be interested in its results.

Summary

In this chapter we discussed the relationship between introducing change in our teaching methods and the institutional and micro-political contexts within which we work. We also suggested that an advantage of the type of insider, own-institute research advocated throughout this book is that, if a democratic approach is adopted, those most affected by its results may 'own' the research and its consequences for their own professional practice. The Appendix explores the use of IT for analyses in qualitative research.

Annotated Reading List and References

Ashcroft, K and Foreman-Peck, L (1994) *Managing Teaching and Learning in Further and Higher Education*, London: Falmer Press.
Addresses issues faced by teachers in managing teaching and learning, drawing throughout on the notion of the reflective practitioner, and contains suggested enquiry tasks related to the issues discussed.

Ashcroft, K, Bigger, S and Coates, D (forthcoming) *Researching into Equal Opportunities in Colleges and Universities*, London: Kogan Page.

Ashcroft, K, Jones, M and Siraj-Blatchford, J (1996) *Researching into Student Learning and Support in Colleges and Universities*, London: Kogan Page.
Explores equal opportunities and related issues and suggests appropriate research tasks using a variety of techniques. This is a volume in the same series as the present book.

Ball, S (1987) *The Micro-Politics of the School: Towards A Theory of School Organization*, London: Methuen.
Explores different organizational and management styles and how teachers can operate effectively within their particular institutional cultures.

Barnett, R (1992) *Improving Higher Education*, Buckingham: Open University Press.
Applies the reflective practitioner model to teaching and learning, arguing for partnership between students and lecturers in critical dialogue about all they think and do as the goal of 'higher' education.

Bell, J (1993) *Doing Your Research Project*, 2nd edn, Buckingham: Open University Press.
A very useful handbook on research design especially intended for first-time researchers in education and social science.

Bennett, N, Crawford, M and Riches, C (1992) *Managing Change in Education: Individual and organizational perspectives*, London: Paul Chapman.
Explores relations between the formulation and implementation of new policies and the strategies used by individuals and groups in response to the different pressures they feel.

Douglas, M (1987) *How Institutions Think*, London: Routledge.
An anthropologist on how institutional cultures influence the thinking of those who belong to them, arguing that different cultures allow individuals to think different kinds of thoughts.

Friedlander, F (1975) 'Emergent and contemporary life-styles; a generational issue', *Human Relations*, 28, 4, 329–47.
Explores relationship between life-style preferences, and management styles.

Earley, P and Fletcher-Campbell, F (1992) 'How are decisions made in departments and schools?', in Bennett, N, Crawford, M and Riches, C (eds) *Managing Change in Education: Individual and organizational perspectives*, London: Paul Chapman, pp.182–201.
Discusses management styles with preference for those which allow for subordinate consultation and participation in decision-making processes.

Gosling, D (1993) 'Informal learning contracts for skills development', in Stephenson, J and Laycock, M (eds) *Using Learning Contracts in Higher Education*, London: Kogan Page, pp.57–69.
Gosling explores the use of informal contracts between tutors and students in helping students to develop and enhance their seminar skills.

Hammersley, M and Atkinson, P (1995) *Ethnography: Principles in practice*, 2nd edn, London: Routledge.
Discusses most aspects of conducting ethnographic research, including recording and analysing as well as ethical issues and the notion of reflexivity. It also explores the problematics of both insider and outsider research.

Handy, C (1988) 'Cultural forces in schools', in Glatter, R, Preedy, M, Riches, C and Masterton, M (eds) *Understanding School Management*, Buckingham: Open University Press, pp.107–16.
Explores different organizational cultures and how they influence those who operate within them, and attract different types of people.

Hoyle, E (1989) 'The micropolitics of schools', in Bush, T (ed.) *Managing Education: Theory and practice*, Buckingham: Open University Press, pp.66–80.
Explores different strategies which managers employ to further their interests and how groups and individuals can operate within various micro-political systems.

Lewis, IM (ed.) (1992) *Social Anthropology in Perspective: The relevance of social anthropology*, Cambridge: Cambridge University Press.
A very readable discussion of the principles and practices of ethnography. It contains historical background and discussion of contemporary issues within the social sciences.

Musgrave, PW (1972) *The Sociology of Education*, 2nd edn, London: University Paperbacks.
A dated but useful discussion of the many social and political factors which impact on the teaching profession from inside and outside the classroom.

Neuman, WL (1994) *Social Research Methods: Quantitative and qualitative approaches*, 2nd edn, Boston, MA: Allyn and Baker.
A very detailed research handbook addressing issues of theory and practice; summary tables and review questions help the reader to engage with the text.

Schon, D (1983) *The Reflective Practitioner: How professionals think in action*, London: Temple Smith.
Suggests that professionals are experts, because knowledge lies in what we do and can not properly be researched by those who only think about but do not practise a profession.

Seymour-Smith, C (1986) *Macmillan Dictionary of Anthropology*, London: Macmillan.
A very useful source of information about central themes and significant contributors within anthropology and the social sciences.

Simons, H (1989) 'Ethics of case study in educational research and evaluation', in Burgess, RG (ed.) *The Ethics of Educational Research*, London: Falmer Press, pp.113–38.
Advocates a democratic approach to insider research which enables participants to own the research and empowers them to take a full part in developing their professional skills.

Slowey, M (1995) *Implementing Change from within Universities*, London: Kogan Page.
Ten accounts of how innovation and change has been managed, sometimes successfully, sometimes not.

Stephenson, J and Laycock, M (eds) (1993) *Using Learning Contracts in Higher Education*, London: Kogan Page.
A very useful book about learning contracts.

Thorley, L and Gregory, R (1994) *Using Group-based Learning in Higher Education*, London: Kogan Page.
Explores how group-based learning can be used to facilitate students' capabilities, confidence and reflective skills, and the tutors' role within this process.

Westoby, A (ed.) (1988) *Culture and Power in Educational Organizations*, Buckingham: Open University Press.
A reader on the politics of educational organizations, designed to enable teachers to operate more effectively within their institutions.

Chapter 6

Series Conclusion: Getting Published

Kate Ashcroft

In this chapter I look at the process of getting published from the publisher's point of view. I outline some of the factors you might consider in choosing a publisher before going on to describe the processes of acceptance, contract and marketing. I then look at issues particular to writing for a journal and discuss the appropriate 'voice' for different types of audience.

Most of this chapter is common to all the books in the series. If you have already read another of the *Practical Research Series*, you may want to skip most of the following sections and go straight to the annotated lists of educational journals, where there will be some journals described that are particular to the topic of this book.

Books from the Publisher's Point of View

Getting started on writing a book is often the hardest part of the process. You need to convince yourself that the things that you know about and that interest you will matter sufficiently to other people to make publication worthwhile, and then you have to get down to it. You may find it reassuring to consider the small scale of much educational publishing. Modern technology has radically reduced the costs of producing a book. This means that sales of a particular book amounting only to 1,000 over two years are no great problem for the publisher. The economies of scale on sales beyond about 2,000 books are not particularly great, so your publisher will be pleased if you become a 'best seller' in academic book terms (sales of about 8,000 books upwards), but will not be disappointed by much more modest sales.

Once you have decided that authorship is for you, you will need to decide a focus for your book or paper. You are likely to have more success if your book is concerned with a current topic or controversial issue, or helps the reader to solve problems. Thus, books or papers that deal with new aspects of a subject (for instance the professional identity of higher education lecturers), with problems that people face in the course of their work or study (such as student diversity), or with a changing situation for which the readers have not been trained (for instance, very large groups of students), are most likely to be welcomed by publishers or editors of journals.

In choosing a topic for a book, there is always a balance to be struck between your needs and those of the reader. For example, you may have completed a research degree in the area of the needs of women returners to higher education and found the subject of your dissertation interesting. However, it is likely to require a complete rewrite and reorientation of the way you approach the subject before it becomes interesting to a larger group of readers.

Publishers receive much unsolicited material through the mail, often in the form of a covering letter and some 'finished' material. Most will consider such approaches carefully. Even so, this is likely to be the least productive way of approaching a publisher. The highest 'hit' rate is likely to be achieved if you are invited to put a proposal forward. Such invitations rarely happen by accident. They often result from putting yourself in the right place at the right time. To do this, you may need to develop networks of contacts. Commissioning editors get to know about potential authors through a number of routes. They attend conferences: you can meet them there and talk to them about your specialist area. They ask influential groups and individuals about likely authors when they perceive a niche in the market: you might get to know the commit-tee members of relevant associations and make sure they know about your potential contribution. They often ask established writers to con-tribute to book series. These 'names' often already have sufficient commissions. If you can get to know established authors, and ensure that they know about you and your interests, they may suggest your name to the editor instead. Commissioning editors also read the educational press, not so much learned journals as papers such as *The Times Educa-tional Supplement, The Times Higher Educational Supplement* and *Education.* If you have written for such papers, your name may become known in the right circles.

Editors also look for pockets of good practice and investigate them for potential authors. If your institution has had an excellent inspection report, or if you are a member of a consortium of colleges or universities that share good practice, you do not have to wait to be discovered. It may be worth drawing an editor's attention to what you are doing and to invite them to talk to you and others about its publishing potential.

I have to admit to never having acted in the ways described above. I received commissions the hard way: by putting a good quality submission to an appropriate publisher. I have been successful when I looked at the process from the editor's point of view. The publisher is much more interested in their readers' needs, and in making a profit, than in your interests. If you can present what you want to do in these terms, you may be successful. This is likely to require some research to find out who your readers are likely to be, how many of them there are, where they will be found, what their interests are and why they will want to buy your particular book. I have been successful in negotiating with publishers when I have approached the writing of a book proposal from this angle.

The publisher will also be interested in the competition for the book you are proposing. If you tell him or her that there is no competition, you are likely to be asked to do more research. If you still cannot find books on your subject, the publisher may worry that there is a good reason why nobody else is publishing in that area. You may be more successful if you undertake a thorough trawl of other publications on topics related to the one that you wish to write about, and then think clearly about your particular selling points and how you can make your book better than the others on the market. Your arguments may vary, depending on what you are writing about. When I co-edited a book on the new National Curriculum, we sold it on the fact that it would be particularly timely (it was to be the first book after the new Orders were published). When I wrote a book on quality and standards, I made sure that it looked at quality issues from the lecturer's point of view (others mainly wrote for institutional managers). In the case of the present series, while there are many books about insider research, and others about aspects of teaching and learning in colleges and universities, there are few that link clear and readable summaries of the current issues into teaching and teaching methods with actual starting points for research in post-compulsory education.

Choosing a Publisher

Once you are clear about what you intend to write and who you are writing for, you will need to choose a publisher. In the UK, there are a relatively small number of publishing houses that specialize in books about education and that are interested in publishing material about further and higher education in particular. Most of the main ones feature in the annotated list of publishers towards the end of this chapter. In addition, there are a number of publishers who are based in other countries, and a number of universities have developed their own small in-house publishing companies.

A few academic authors use a literary agent. If you wish to do so, the *Artists and Writers Year Book* will help you locate an appropriate one. The agent will place your book with an appropriate publisher, do most of the negotiation on your behalf, act as a critical friend, take care of the bookkeeping, correspondence and so on. The academic book market works with low profit margins. For this reason royalty schemes are fairly inflexible. Once you have paid his or her fees, using a literary agent is unlikely to mean that you make much more money.

If you decide to go it alone, you may find it useful to look around at the booklists of various publishers to find those that have a sizeable list in your subject. It is easier to market a group of books with a common theme. If a publisher is advertising a book series in the area of teaching and teaching methods in tertiary education, they may be more likely to look seriously at your proposal. The next stage is to look at publishers' house-styles: the appearance of the books, the type of print and lay out, and the usual length and format of the books they produce. You will also have to decide whether to go for a large publishing house or a smaller, more specialized one. Larger houses have the marketing facilities to promote books across the world. On the other hand, junior editors in large houses have little power and may take some time to get approval for action. Small publishing houses may give more personal service. They also tend to be more highly specialized and so know a lot about publishing in a particular field.

Once you have narrowed your options, it may be useful to ask colleagues, booksellers and librarians about the reputation and efficiency of those publishing houses that remain on your list, before making an approach to one or more publisher. If you are new to writing for publication, it is probably worth telephoning likely publishing houses to talk to the commissioning editor for post-compulsory education or making contact with publishing representatives at conferences.

You can then talk about your ideas to see if he or she is interested in them. Generally, the commissioning editor will be happy to provide you with guidelines on how to submit a formal proposal. Provided you let them know you are doing so, publishers generally do not object if you submit your book outline to two or three houses.

Once you have found a publisher you feel you can do business with, you may decide to meet. Publishing seems to be a business that thrives on personal relationships If you deal with a publisher by letter, you may build a relationship quicker if you use their name, rather than 'sir' or 'madam'.

If the commissioning editor likes your proposal, he or she will usually ask for reports from a couple of referees. The referees' reports often contain suggestions for change. Try not to be discouraged by this. It is not at all unusual to be asked for clarification, more information or slight changes before a proposal is accepted. This process can improve the proposal considerably. When I first put forward the proposal for this book series it included many more shorter books. My editor made several suggestions and I reworked the series proposals twice before we were both convinced that it was as sound as it could be.

Negotiating the Contract

Once it looks like you are more or less 'in business', you will need to discuss terms and conditions. The level of royalties offered by academic publishers does not vary greatly, but it is always worth trying to negotiate a slightly better deal or asking for a small advance on royalties, especially if you are involved in some immediate expenses (for instance, a new computer or photographic material). Whatever terms you eventually agree, it is important to read your contract carefully. Most are fairly standard. You may be paid royalties as a percentage of the net price. On the other hand, especially if your book is of the type that may be sold at a discount (for instance, through book clubs), your royalties may be a percentage of net receipts (what the publishing house actually receives from sales). This arrangement allows the publisher to pay you a lower amount per book sold, where the books are sold at a discount. If you are editing a book with chapters contributed by others, the publishing house may pay the chapter authors a small fee on publication. The total of these fees may then be set against your royalties.

Copyright may be held by the publisher or the author. In practice, this may make little difference, as, in any case, the publisher will normally reserve exclusive publishing rights. In other cases the small print on contracts can be important. For instance, I would never sign a contract that gave the publisher an option on subsequent books.

Your contract is likely to say that the publisher reserves the right not to publish your book if you deliver it after a fixed date or if it is of poor quality. In practice, these clauses are not often invoked. Provided you have let your editor know in advance of the deadline, she or he will usually be willing to allow some slippage. If it does not come up to expectations, she or he will also usually help you to improve the book, rather than abandon it altogether. There will usually be a clause in the contract about excess correction charges.

It is in your interests to undertake careful proof-reading at the early stages. Once the book has been typeset, substantial changes late in the process can have knock-on effects you may not have anticipated: for instance, the indexing may need to be redone. Do not forget to check the spelling on the title pages. I have heard of a spelling mistake that was found on the cover after binding; as a consequence, the author lost several hundred pounds in royalties.

One decision you will have to make is whether to do your own indexing. Most publishers have links with professional indexers who will do this job for you for a charge that is set against royalties. Professional indexers usually do a sound job, but they may not know the subject area as well you do. If you decide to do your own index, your editor should be able to provide you with guidelines on house-style and give you tips to make the job relatively painless (for instance, using a highlighter on a photocopy at the proof-reading stage to mark significant words and phrases). Indexing computer programs exist that can simplify the job a little.

Your relationship with your editor is likely to develop over time. Many authors stick with one editor for a considerable period. This relationship will be much easier if you are the sort of person who meets deadlines. Your editor is more likely to work hard on behalf of a cooperative and efficient author who answers correspondence promptly and delivers on time. Because the unexpected always occurs, I always aim to complete the book well before the agreed deadline.

Good time management requires planning from the start. It may be useful to audit your position, to look at your commitments and decide what it is possible to do and to allow some leeway in your schedule. I am always disconcerted by the amount of time finishing a book takes. The process of checking references, tidying headings, creating the table of contents and so on takes a lot of time. When you submit the manuscript, you need to be prepared for more work. The publisher may send you a marked-up manuscript to check before typesetting. If so, it is important that you have set aside the time to do a thorough job. This will be the last chance to make substantial changes. After the manuscript has been typeset, you will be asked to undertake thorough and careful proof-reading. At the same time, it is likely that you will be approached by the marketing department with requests for a range of information to help the publisher to sell the book. This is an important stage, and one to which you should give time and thought. It is probably a good idea to talk through the post-submission schedule with your publisher, so that you can blank out some days in your diary to do all this work.

The marketing of your book is partially your responsibility. The low profit margin on academic books means that your book is unlikely to be advertised in the press (unless it is part of a series that may be included in a composite advertisement). A few books will be sent out for review. If you expect to see your book described in the educational press during the following months, you may be disappointed. Not all books sent for review will be included and, even where they are, the review may not be printed for up to a year. Much marketing takes place through direct mail shots. The publicity department will need your help in targeting these. Another important marketing outlet is the conference circuit. You will need to inform the marketing department of key events where publicity about your book should be available. If you are giving a paper at a conference, you should make sure that your book is on prominent display. Do not be afraid to act as a shameless self-publicist.

Writing for a Journal

The most usual way of getting started in publishing is to write for a newspaper or journal. If you submit articles for the educational press, you will be up against stiff competition from professional journalists. Unless you have already established a name within education, you may find it a difficult field to break into. You may be more likely to succeed if your article has something special that will catch the editor's attention. This 'something' may be topicality, controversy or human interest. If your area of enquiry has started to feature as a national issue (for example, the switch to semesterization or the introduction of transfer-able skills in higher education), it is worth submitting a timely article to the educational press. If what you want to say is of direct application or relevance to the reader (for instance, an aspect of the use of IT packages that has immediate classroom application), it may be publishable. On the whole, the educational press wants interesting articles, written in a short and non-technical way. It may not be interested in straightforward research reports.

Journals are likely to be more interested in the sort of research and enquiry that we have been suggesting in this series. You are unlikely to be paid for a paper or article in a journal, but this form of publishing can make a good starting point for a would-be academic author. Once you have completed your thinking, reading, research and/or enquiry, ideally you should start to consider the journals that might accept it before you start writing so that you can adapt your style to their requirements. I must admit that I have never taken this advice. I always write what I want to say, in my own style, and then look round for a journal that seems as if it might welcome that sort of paper. Whatever approach you take, you need to be aware that different journals carry various amounts of prestige in the world of education. This status is not an objective thing and is best ascertained by asking around your colleagues and fellow academic writers.

On the whole, you will achieve more status and professional recognition if you publish in a refereed journal, especially if it reaches an international audience. The refereeing process means that the quality of your paper is subjected to scrutiny by (usually two) outside experts, before it is published. They will often suggest that you should change your paper in various ways. You may want to consider these requests very seriously, since they are usually made by people who know a great deal about the subject and about writing. On the other hand, the paper is yours, and you may decide not to agree to changes if that would make the paper say things that you disagree with or fundamentally change the tone you wished to take.

More status is accorded to publication in very well-established journals. On the other hand, they tend to have a large number of experienced writers who regularly write for them: your paper will compete for space with many experts. You may stand a better chance of being published if you submit to a relatively new publication. My first paper appeared in the (then) new international journal *Assessment and Evaluation in Higher Education* that has now grown into a very well respected publication. If you start with a new journal, and if you both do well, you can build a long-lasting relationship to your mutual benefit.

The frequency of publication may be another factor in your choice of journal. Journals that appear only once or twice a year may not deal with your paper expeditiously. Since it is generally not 'done' to send your paper to several journals at the same time, this can be a real problem. A journal that publishes more regularly will probably referee and publish your paper more quickly. This is especially important if your paper is on a topical theme.

You will find detailed guidance at the back of most journals on how the editors need you to set out your manuscript, references and so on. It will generally explain the usual length of acceptable articles and the number of copies of the manuscript that must be sent. It is important to keep to these guidelines.

Finding your Voice

When you start writing you will need to find your own style. On the whole it may be better for inexperienced writers to keep their style serious but simple. It is tempting to try to sound more authoritative by a 'mock posh' or passive way of writing. This is usually a mistake. Straightforward reporting, using as little jargon and as few conditional clauses as is consistent with the complexity of your subject matter, will probably work best.

The unique selling point of your book will influence the register and style of your writing. If you are writing for a highly specialized readership, with a wealth of expert knowledge and experience of reading difficult texts, you may get away with a more dense and complex writing style. On the other hand, if you are writing for undergraduate students, or busy lecturers or teachers, simple English with short sentences and paragraphs may communicate better. You will need to avoid being pompous but also to take into account that books are different from letters and newspaper articles, and need a slightly more formal style. Written language is quite different from verbal communication. 'Conversational' styles of writing can come across as patronizing or unintelligent. For this reason, it is hard to bring off jokes or rhetorical questions in academic writing.

Gradually, you should learn to recognize your strengths and weaknesses. This awareness builds painfully over time. One of my own particular faults is that I can be too didactic. I now look through my work for imperatives, such as 'ought', 'must' and 'should' to check that I would not be better to replace them with more tentative words, such as 'might' or 'may' that imply that the reader has some choice in interpreting what I am suggesting. I also ask a few colleagues to read through anything I am submitting for publication and to be as critical and demanding as possible. I find that I have to write and rewrite up to 20 times before everyone is satisfied.

Annotated List of Educational Publishers

Below I have listed many of the major publishers which are interested in books and/or curriculum materials to support teaching and learning within colleges and universities.

Cassell, Wellington House, 125 Strand, London WC2R 0BB. Telephone: 0171 420 5555.
Cassell publishes books aimed at teachers and undergraduate and postgraduate students of education and at the general market. The books reflect the most recent research into education, psychology and related academic subjects. While being at the cutting edge, they should also be clearly written and accessible. They are frequently aimed at the international market, while covering the most up-to-date policy developments in the UK.

The most recent editorial strategy is to publish a series of high level books of debates that feature international scholars.

David Fulton, 2 Barbon Close, Great Ormond Street, London WC1N 3JX. Telephone: 0171 405 5656.
David Fulton specializes in publishing within education, with a focus towards teachers of students and children with profound and multiple learning difficulties. It also publishes much for initial teacher education. It is hoping to build from this very strong base a list that covers other issues in the college and university sector.

It mainly publishes books which, while grounded in current research or classroom practice, set out lessons and issues for people to use in their professional practice or in their studies. It does not publish research *per se*, nor publish exclusively for the academic community.

It is a good publishing firm for a new author, since it will provide a personal service that includes much support and encouragement. In addition, its average turn around time from manuscript to finished book is under five months.

Falmer Press, 4 John Street, London WC1N 2ET. Telephone: 0171 405 2237.
Falmer is a large and prestigious educational publisher. Once it has accepted your proposal, it will allow you to get on with your writing with little interference. This has the advantage for experienced writers of allowing much freedom, but does require that you are disciplined and know what you are doing.

Its list covers a wide variety of age ranges and subjects within education, including books on adolescence, equal opportunities, curriculum, educational policy and management, the disciplines of education, subject teaching, teacher education and student learning. The books are authoritative and well researched. They are aimed at students, practitioners and academics.

Framework Press, Parkfield, Greaves Road, Lancaster, LA1 4TZ. Telephone: 01524 39602.
This is a small, specialist publisher that is particularly interested in interactive curriculum and development materials. Much of its output is in the form of student-centred, activity-based material, in a ring-bound, photocopiable format (although it occasionally publishes books). The audiences that it caters for include students, teachers and educational mangers. The list covers school and college management; staff development within schools, colleges and universities; vocational material, especially related to GNVQs; and curriculum material for English and Personal Social Education. The commissioning editor is interested in material covering all aspects of teaching and teaching methods. If you are thinking of creating materials that will allow your readership to interact and to do things, rather than to take away and read, this may be the outlet for you.

Further Education Development Agency, Publications Department, Coombe Lodge, Blagdon, Bristol BS18 6RG. Telephone: 01761 462503.
This new agency is developing a publication list that will cover a variety of aspects of teaching, learning, assessment and management, focusing particularly on the further education sector.

Heinemann, Halley Court, Jordan Hill, Oxford OX2 8EJ. Telephone: 01865 311366.
Heinemann is one of the major educational publishers. Its list covers a wide variety of aspects of teaching in the university and college sector.

Hodder and Stoughton, 338 Euston Road, London NW1 3BH. Telephone: 0171 873 6000.
Hodder and Stoughton Educational covers a wide range of subjects for further and higher education, including business, health and caring, catering, beauty therapy and vocational languages. At the higher education level, it has a teacher education list with a strongly practical focus, some of which is published in cooperation with the Open University.
    Most of its publishing is taken up with core and supplementary textbooks, supported by teacher packs and student-centred workbooks. Its language publishing is fully supported by audio packs, with prize-winning CD-ROMs accompanying some courses.

Jessica Kingsley, 116 Pentonville Road, London N1 9JB. Telephone: 0171 833 2307.
Jessica Kingsley publishes books mainly for professionals. It asks authors

to bear in mind that the essence of the sort of publishing that it does is a combination of theory and practice.

In the educational field, at school level it specializes in special educational needs, pastoral care and educational psychology. At further and higher education level, it publishes a series of books on management and policy. These include books on broad issues, such as quality in further education, and books with a narrower focus, such as the use of information technology in education management.

Kogan Page, 120 Pentonville Road, London N1 9JN. Telephone: 0171 278 0433.

Kogan Page is a large and well-respected publisher. It is always looking for book proposals in management and leadership, initial teacher education, mentoring, open and distance learning, learning theory, vocational education, research and assessment. It is always prepared to look at new areas if the proposal is good.

The further and higher education commissioning editor points out that authors who follow the Kogan Page guidelines and do the background research are more likely to get a positive response or at least constructive criticism which will help develop the book. She also points out that many people do not do the background research to find out if a publisher is interested in a particular area and this accounts for a large number of rejections.

Macmillan, Brunel Road, Houndmills, Basingstoke RG21 2XS. Telephone: 01256 29242.

Macmillan does not publish extensively in the field of education. It does however publish a range of study skill books for students.

Multilingual Matters, Frankfurt Lodge, Clevedon Hall, Victoria Road, Clevedon BS21 7SJ. Telephone: 01275 876519.

It specializes in books related to multicultural and anti-racist education.

Open University Press, Cedric Court, 22 Billmoor, Buckingham MK18 1XW. Telephone: 01280 823388.

Open University Press publishes a range of textbooks in conjunction with the Society for Research into Higher Education for academics worldwide in their generic professional roles as teachers, researchers and managers. It currently publishes books in four fields (which can and do overlap):

- Planning and management: books about leadership, strategic management, human resource management, financial management and so on, for managers and aspiring managers in colleges and universities.
- Teaching, counselling and learning: books for academics in their role as teachers and tutors, for new lecturers and all lecturers who wish to reflect upon and improve their teaching.

- History and philosophy: specialist monographs, appealing to scholars of, and researchers into, the worlds of further and higher education.
- Policy and context: this includes books of interest across the further and higher education sector, including books on funding arrangements, quality assurance, enterprise and equal opportunities.

Open University Press is particularly interested in an international audience. Interested authors are invited to apply to John Shelton at the Open University Press for a book proposal guide.

Oxford University Press, Walton Street, Oxford OX2 6DP. Telephone: 01856 56767.
Oxford University Press does not specialize in education, but it is interested in books in the area of political and social studies, especially books for students, including undergraduate and postgraduate students of education. These books tend to be related to the disciplines of education (for instance, psychology and sociology). It also has a management list for academics and would be interested in books in the area of educational management and for the general public.
It has no standard format for book proposals.

Pergamon Press, Elsevier Science Ltd, The Boulevard, Langford Lane, Kidlington OX5 1GB. Telephone: 01865 843000.
Pergamon Press has a small education list. It is currently interested in books covering issues in higher education. These books tend to be authoritatively written contributions to controversies in higher education, written from a cross-national point of view. Studies in the series are each based on comparisons between at least two countries. The intended audience includes educational managers, administrators, teachers, researchers and students.
Prospective authors are invited to contact Professor Guy Neave, International Association of Universities.

Routledge, 11 New Fetter Lane, London EC4P 4EE. Telephone: 0171 583 9855.
Routledge has an extensive educational list that includes educational management, teaching students with special educational needs and open and distance learning. Its list covers all aspects of teaching and learning, and further and higher education and the disciplines in education.

Scottish Academic Press, 56 Hanover Street, Edinburgh EH2 2DX. Telephone: 0131 255 7483.
Scottish Academic Press publishes a range of books on education, mostly with a Scottish flavour. It aims to publish scholarly works in every field of study and research. Its list covers the full age range and includes books on assessment, subject teaching, curriculum development, management issues, educational policy, comparative education, Scottish educational history, student learning and teacher education.

Staff and Educational Development Association, Gala House, 3 Raglan Road, Edgbaston, Birmingham B57 RA. Telephone: 0121 4405021.
The Staff and Educational Development Association (SEDA) publishes SEDA Papers in the form of short A4 books and is also cooperating with Kogan Page to produce a series of books on teaching in universities.

SEDA Papers are published for a mainly UK audience and may be edited collections or authored books. You will not have to provide an index, and you should use accessible language. The Papers tend to be published in small print runs and you will not receive royalties or expenses.

The book series contains books of around 60,000 words long and are written for an international audience. They may be edited collections or authored books. Again, royalties go to SEDA.

Sally Brown, Educational Development Service, University of Northumbria at Newcastle, Newcastle upon Tyne NE1 8ST, Telephone 0191 227 3985 will be happy to talk to you informally about your proposal or to send you some guidelines for authors.

Technical and Educational Services, Ravenswood Road, Bristol BS6 6BW.
It has a small list, mainly by the same group of authors, focused on helpful hints for higher education teachers.

Annotated List of Education Journals

The list of journals below includes the name of the journal, the publisher, the frequency of publication and the name and address of the editor(s) to whom material for publication should be sent. These details were sent to me by the publishers at the time of writing, but, since editors can move on and (less frequently) editorial policies can change, you might be wise to check before you embark on publication. Most of the journals will also accept book reviews, shorter discussion papers and research summaries.

Association for Learning Technology Journal
Association for Learning Technology. Published twice a year.
Manuscripts to: G Jacob, School of European Languages, University College, Swansea SA2 8PP.
A new international journal concerned with research and reports of good practice in the development and use of all kinds of learning technology in higher education. Some of the language is clearly designed to communicate with experts in information technology, but much of the content is directly concerned with insider research and student learning.

British Educational Research Journal
　　Carfax. Published quarterly.
　　Manuscripts to: G Weiner, Department of Education, South Bank
　　Polytechnic, Caxton House, 13–16 Borough Road, London SE1 0AL.
　　This well-established international journal is interdisciplinary in
　　approach. It includes reports of experiments, qualitative research as well
　　as conceptual papers and articles concerned with methodological issues.
　　The focus is on research, but the approach is very eclectic.

British Journal of Educational Studies
　　Blackwell. Published quarterly.
　　Manuscripts to: D Halpin, Institute of Education, University of Warwick,
　　Coventry CV4 7AL.
　　A well-established refereed journal that is concerned with discussion of
　　basic principles and topics of major importance or topicality. The papers
　　reflect a variety of perspectives and disciplines, but the journal is not
　　generally interested in reports of empirical research. Many of the papers
　　are by established 'names' in education and most are of a conceptual
　　nature. This is not the place for insider research, but it would be worth
　　considering if you wanted to discuss issues relevant to the educational
　　system in general.

British Journal of In-Service Education
　　Triangle. Published three times a year.
　　Manuscripts to: M Lee, University College of Bretton Hall, Wakefield,
　　West Yorkshire WF4 4LG.
　　This refereed, well-established international journal publishes papers
　　about inservice education in its widest sense. This includes staff
　　development projects within universities and colleges. It is interested in
　　discussion of new issues and reports of research and developments. Some
　　of the research papers included are wide-ranging in scope, but others
　　involve theory emerging from smaller studies.

Cambridge Journal of Education
　　Triangle. Published three times a year.
　　Manuscripts to: B Shannon, University of Cambridge Institute of
　　Education, Shaftesbury Road, Cambridge CB2 2BX.
　　This journal welcomes research reports and other types of paper that
　　span the divide between teacher and researcher. It is therefore a good
　　starting point if you are looking for an outlet for insider research. The
　　papers are fairly short, generally accessible and highly eclectic in subject
　　matter.

Curriculum Studies
　　Triangle. Published three times a year.
　　Manuscripts to: W Carr, Division of Education, University of Sheffield,
　　388 Glossop Road, Sheffield S10 2JA.

This is a fairly new international journal that seeks to stimulate debate between different cultures and societies. It draws on perspectives beyond those usually represented in learned journals. It welcomes interdisciplinary, eclectic papers, especially where they link policy and practice. If your enquiry or discussion includes curriculum initiatives, and you have looked at the perspectives of various of the stakeholders in education, this may be a particularly good outlet for you.

Education Today
Pitman. Published quarterly.
Manuscripts to: The Editor, College of Preceptors, Coppice Row, Theydon Bois, Epping CM16 7DN.
This journal is a forum for debate, although it does include some educational research. The statement of educational policy does not go beyond this, and I have not been able to discern any other features of policy from the very eclectic nature of the papers.

Educational Research
Routledge. Published three times a year.
Manuscripts to: S Hegarty, National Foundation for Educational Research, The Mere, Upton Park, Slough, Berks SL1 1DP.
This is the official journal of the National Foundation for Educational Research and is principally a forum for reporting research projects and reviews of research. It is particularly interested in contemporary issues and publishes papers reporting experiments or surveys, most of which include large samples.

Educational Action Research
Triangle. Published three times a year.
Manuscripts to: Dr B Somekh, Centre for Applied Research in Education, School of Education, University of East Anglia, Norwich NR4 7TJ.
This fairly new refereed journal welcomes accounts of action research and development studies and also conceptual or empirical pieces that contribute to the debate on action research and associated methodologies. It looks for readability and the recognition of the problematic nature of educational knowledge. It is a particularly appropriate vehicle for reports of insider research that are honest about the difficulties and the emotional context of enquiry. Because the journal wishes to foster practitioner research, if the editors decide that they cannot publish your work, they will generally provide suggestions as to how it might be improved.

Educational Review
Carfax. Published three times a year.
Manuscripts to: The Editors, School of Education, University of Birmingham, Edgbaston, Birmingham B15 2TT.
This well-established refereed journal publishes a range of articles and research. It is particularly interested in research, much of it quantitative,

but includes some discussion papers. It tends to be focused on schools rather than post-compulsory education.

Educational Studies
Carfax. Published three times a year.
Manuscripts to: D Cherrington, International Centre for Advanced Studies, Cheltenham and Gloucester College of Higher Education, Cheltenham GL50 2EB.
This well-established journal aims to provide a forum for original investigations and theoretical studies in education. It is principally concerned with research in the social science tradition, much of it experimental research.

Evaluation and Research in Education
Multilingual Matters. Published three times a year.
Manuscripts to: K Morrison, School of Education, University of Durham, Leazes Road, Durham DH1 1TA.
This journal aims to make methods of evaluation and research available to teachers, administrators and research workers. It includes evaluation and research reports, conceptual and methodological papers and papers that look at the implications of the above for action. There is a heavy focus on the rationale for various types of evaluation, discussion of its theoretical framework and methodological analysis.

Evaluation Practice
JAI Press. Published three times a year.
Manuscripts to: M Smith, 2115 Symons Hall, University of Maryland, College Park, MD 20742, USA.
This international refereed journal takes contributions from any discipline. It speaks to professional evaluators, but looks at improving practice and skill as well as knowledge. It covers a broad range of topics and is interested in promoting dialogue. It has space for long and highly technical papers, but also for shorter discussion papers.

Higher Education Policy
Kogan Page. Published quarterly.
Manuscripts to: International Association of Universities, Unesco House, 1 rue Miollis, 75732 Paris Cedex 15, France.
This international journal is the quarterly journal of the International Association of Universities. This association sees its role as promoting the principles of freedom and justice, of human dignity and solidarity at an international, national and regional level. It is therefore interested in papers that address problems of that kind. It looks for well-sourced papers that express controversial or provocative opinions and expert reviews of new developments, such as systems reform.

Higher Education Quarterly
Blackwell. Published quarterly.

Manuscripts to: M Shattock, Senate House, University of Warwick, Coventry CV4 7AL.

The editorial policy is not stated in the journal and so I have inferred it from the papers it contains. These seem to be concerned with the debate about higher education, its aims and purposes and the ways the system as a whole and the individual institution are influenced by powerful groups and ideas in society. At the moment, the principal preoccupations seem to be quality assessment and funding. If you have done some research at the level of the institution as a whole, or have a well-documented argument to put forward about the direction in which the system is moving, this journal might provide a useful outlet for publication.

Higher Education Review

Tyrrell Burgess Associates. Published three times a year.
Manuscripts to: J Pratt, 46 Merers Road, London N19 4PR.

This international journal speaks to the research community in post-compulsory education and welcomes papers that give a critique of developments in this area. It includes some traditional research reports, but also papers that look at broad issues in education.

Innovation and Learning in Education: The International Journal for the Reflective Practitioner

MCB University Press. Published three times a year.
Manuscripts to: G McElwee, School of Management, University of Humberside, Cottingham Road, Hull HU6 7RT.

This is a new journal committed to a critical evaluation of teaching, learning and related issues in post-compulsory education. It is looking for papers that bridge the gap between theory and practice, and as such it is a good vehicle for the kind of insider research that is located within a theoretical framework. It is particularly interested in exploring the ways that teaching and learning may be enhanced within a context of reducing resources. It seeks to share good practice, stimulate and encourage debate and enhance teaching and learning. It is looking for papers from a variety of 'insiders': teachers, course leaders, mangers and others. Papers tend to be short (up to 3,000 words). They are often broken up by sub-headings and diagrams. The language of the papers tends to be fairly non-academic and reader-friendly.

Innovations in Education and Training International

Kogan Page. Published quarterly.
Manuscripts to: C Bell, University of Plymouth, Plymouth PL4 8AA.

This journal is a relaunch of *Education and Training Technology International*. It is interested in papers that would help practitioners and managers keep abreast of innovations and update their skills. It publishes refereed papers, case studies and papers based on opinion. The important criterion is that material submitted should reflect the state of the art in education and training. The journal is published in cooperation with major UK staff development associations and reflects their priority of direct application to practice This makes it a particularly appropriate vehicle for insider research, especially if it involves the use of technology.

Interchange

Kluwer. Published three times a year.

Manuscripts to: L Lenz, Faculty of Education, University of Calgary, 2500 University Drive NW, Toronto, Ontario T2N 1N4, Canada.

This refereed international journal is concerned with educational theory, research, educational history, philosophy, policy and practice. It seeks to promote exchange between practitioners, policy makers and scholars. It looks for frank, argumentative papers on the fundamental purposes of education. Most of the papers are firmly embedded in a review of the international literature.

Journal of Education for Teaching

Carfax. Published three times a year.

Manuscripts to: E Stones, 11 Serpentine Road, Selly Park, Birmingham B29 7HU.

This well-established international refereed journal has achieved a high status by taking a fairly limited and traditional view of what is acceptable as 'research'. It is a particularly scholarly journal that welcomes discussions on new issues and research reports, particularly in the quantitative tradition. Where it accepts qualitative research, it seems to favour a quasi-experimental research design.

Journal of Further and Higher Education

NATFHE. Published three times a year.

Manuscripts to: A Castling, c/o NATFHE, 27 Britannia Street, London WC1X 9JP.

A highly eclectic journal that includes a number of fairly short papers. The editorial policy is not stated, but there appears to be a heavy emphasis on discussion of equal opportunities and vocational preparation.

Journal of Information Technology for Teacher Education

Triangle. Published three times a year.

Manuscripts to: B Robinson, Department of Education, University of Cambridge, 17 Trumpington Street, Cambridge CB2 1QA.

This well-established international, refereed journal is concerned with all aspects of information technology within pre- and inservice teacher education. In general, the papers are rather oriented to school and university teacher education departments, but if you have undertaken a staff or course development project involving technology, you might find this a useful outlet. The tone of the papers varies from reader-friendly to highly technical. The scope of many of the papers is limited and includes some insider research reports.

Journal of Teacher Development
Pitman. Published quarterly.
Manuscripts to: M Golby, School of Education, Exeter University,
Heavitree Road, Exeter EX1 2LU.
This journal particularly welcomes articles from practitioners. Papers
include small-scale research and personal responses to policy initiatives.
They tend to be focused on schools and teacher education departments
of universities, but some from other contexts are included. This might be
a good outlet to report on staff development projects or policy issues
within staff development.

New Academic
SEDA. Published three times a year.
Manuscripts to: E Mapstone, St Yse, St Nectan's Glen, Tintagel, Cornwall
PL34 0BE.
This looks like a magazine but is a new refereed journal. Its aim is to
promote good practice in teaching and a better understanding of the
processes involved in higher education. The readership is drawn from a
wide range of disciplines, and is therefore a non-specialist audience. It
welcomes clear, straightforward accounts of research and practice, written
(despite the title) in non-academic English. Articles tend to be very short:
from less than one to three A4 pages, often with photographs or simple
diagrams. This would be a good place to report a small-scale evaluation of
your practice, written in such a way that the lessons applicable to other
contexts are brought out.

Oxford Review of Education
Carfax. Published three times a year.
Manuscripts to: D Phillips, University of Oxford Department of
Educational Studies, 15 Norham Gardens, Oxford OX2 6PY.
Many of the papers in this journal are speculative or concern the
elaboration and evaluation of empirical theory about the improvement of
practice. Not all papers include original research; some are reviews of the
research to date, others are analyses of policy initiatives and their results.
The style and the literature base that underpin the articles are quite
varied.

Qualitative Studies in Education
Taylor and Francis. Published four times a year.
Manuscripts to: S Ball, Centre for Educational Studies, King's College
London, 552 King's Road, London SW10 0UA.
This fairly new international journal publishes papers that employ a
variety of qualitative methods and approaches including ethnographic
enquiry, history, grounded theory, biography, case studies and curriculum
criticism. The papers address educational issues of interest to a wide
audience and report naturalistic data that have been systematically
analysed. Papers focus on school, college, university and work-place
settings as well as on research methods and ethics.

RESEARCHING TEACHING METHODS

Research Papers in Education
Routledge. Published three times a year.
Manuscripts to: P Preece, School of Education, University of Exeter, St Lukes, Heavitree Road, Exeter EX1 2LA.
This journal publishes papers that have particular relevance for policy and practice in education. It publishes full and detailed accounts of research and also looks for up-to-date and authoritative articles. It specializes in very long papers reporting research projects in full.

Studies in Educational Evaluation
Pergamon. Published quarterly.
Manuscripts to: A Lewy, School of Education, Tel Aviv University, Tel Aviv, Israel; M Alkin, Graduate School, of Education, UCLA, Los Angeles, CA 90024, USA; B McGaw, Australian Council of Educational Research, PO Box 210, Hawthorne, Victoria 3122, Australia; or R Langeheine, Institute for Science Education (IPN), University of Kiel, Germany.
This well-established, international journal publishes original reports of evaluation. These include fairly rigorous empirical studies and theoretical reflections on evaluation. It also publishes discursive pieces about the state of the art in various contexts, subjects or countries. On the whole, the tone of the papers is scholarly. If your investigations have led to you conceptualize evaluation processes in a new way or if you have been able to undertake a fairy extensive empirical research study, it might be a good place to publish.

Studies in Higher Education
Society for Research into Higher Education/Carfax. Published quarterly.
Manuscripts to: R Barnett, Centre for Higher Education Studies, Department of Policy, Institute of Education, 55–59 Gordon Square, London WC1H ONT.
This well-established international journal publishes research that illuminates teaching and learning by bringing to bear disciplinary perspectives. It also welcomes papers about teachers' reflections on their own practice. The papers are well written, accessible, but rigorous. It includes empirical research and more discursive papers that are often based on an extensive review of the literature.

Teachers and Teaching: Theory and Practice
Carfax. Published three times a year.
Manuscripts to: C Day, ISATT, University of Nottingham, University Park, Nottingham, NG7 2RD.
This new publication is the journal of the International Study Association on Teacher Thinking. It aims to provide an international focal point for the publication of debate, completed research and research in progress on teachers and teaching and, in particular, on teacher thinking. It accepts qualitative and quantitative studies as well as reflective and analytical papers. The intended audience is policy makers, academics,

118

teacher educators and teachers within education and the caring professions. If you are interested in publishing a paper on any aspect of the 'inner life' of the teacher: personal and practical knowledge; values and beliefs; attitudes; dilemmas; biographies; curriculum thinking; or professional action, this may an appropriate outlet.

Teaching in Higher Education
Carfax. Published three times a year.
Manuscripts to: L Barton, Division of Education, University of Sheffield, Sheffield S10 2TN.
This is a new international refereed journal that looks at the roles of teaching, learning and the curriculum in higher education. It is seeking research papers and discursive articles that critically examine the values and assumptions that underpin teaching, identify new agendas for research, develop international comparative insights or consider the link between teaching and research. If it develops along similar lines to other journals edited by Len Barton, you will need to ensure that any paper you submit is securely located within the international literature.

Tertiary Education and Management
Jessica Kingsley. Published twice a year.
Manuscripts to: NR Begg, The University of Aberdeen, Aberdeen.
This new journal is intended for professionals in the area of higher education management, and for academics researching that area. It aims to publish keynote and contributed papers of high quality of interest to European educationalists and the profession.

The Vocational Aspects of Education
Triangle. Published three times a year.
Manuscripts to: B Bailey, School of Post-compulsory Education and Training, University of Greenwich, Avery Hill Road, Eltham, London SE9 2HB.
This journal publishes papers related to vocational education and training. It is looking for overtly 'scholarly' papers that address the development and theory of vocational education, wherever it occurs. The language of many of the articles is fairly technical, and there is a heavy emphasis on the location of discourse within a theoretical framework. This may be a better bet for discursive pieces than for insider research reports.

Westminster Studies in Education
Carfax. Published annually.
Manuscripts to: WF Fearon, Westminster College, Oxford OX2 9AT.
This well-established journal looks for unconventional papers. If you want to explore a neglected area, or put forward an unusual viewpoint, particularly if the style you choose is discursive and reflective, this may be the journal for you.

If your paper covers a specialist area, journals that you may wish to look at include the following.

Assessment and Evaluation in Higher Education
    Carfax. Published three times a year.
    Manuscripts to: WAH Scott, School of Education, University of Bath.

Assessment in Education: Principles, Policy and Practice
    Carfax. Published three times a year.
    Manuscripts to: P Broadfoot, School of Education, University of Bristol.

British Journal of Educational Psychology
    British Psychological Society. Published quarterly.
    Manuscripts to: M Youngman, School of Education, University of Nottingham.

British Journal of Music Education
    Cambridge University Press. Published three times a year.
    Manuscripts to: J Paynter, University of York, or K Swanwick, University of London Institute of Education.

British Journal of Religious Education
    Alden Press. Published three times a year.
    Manuscripts to: JM Hall, University of Birmingham.

British Journal of Sociology of Education
    Carfax. Published quarterly.
    Manuscripts to: L Barton, Division of Education, University of Sheffield.

Comparative Education
    Carfax. Published three times a year.
    Manuscripts to: P Broadfoot, University of Bristol.

Compare: A Journal of Comparative Education
    Carfax. Published three times a year.
    Manuscripts to: C Brock, University of Oxford.

Curriculum Inquiry
    Blackwell. Published quarterly.
    Manuscripts to: FM Connolly, The Ontario Institute for Studies in Education.

The Curriculum Journal
    Routledge. Published three times a year.
    Manuscripts to: M James, University of Cambridge Institute of Education.

Computers and Education
    Pergamon. Published eight times a year.
    Manuscripts to: MR Kibby, University of Strathclyde.

Disability and Society
Carfax. Published quarterly.
Manuscripts to: L Barton, Division of Education, University of Sheffield.

Education Economics
Carfax. Published three times a year.
Manuscripts to: G Johnes, Lancaster University.

Educational Management and Administration
Pitman. Published quarterly.
Manuscripts to: P Ribbins, Centre for Education Management and Policy
Studies, School of Education, University of Birmingham.

Educational Psychology
Carfax. Published quarterly.
Manuscripts to: R Riding, University of Birmingham.

Educational Studies in Mathematics
Kluwer. Published four times yearly.
Manuscripts to: Kluwer, Dordrecht, The Netherlands.

Educational Theory
University of Illinois. Published four times yearly.
Manuscripts to: NC Burbules, University of Illinois, USA.

Environmental Education Research
Carfax. Published three times a year.
Manuscripts to: C Oulton, University of Bath.

European Journal of Education
Carfax. Published quarterly.
Manuscripts to: The Editors, European Institute of Education and Social
Policy, Université de Paris.

European Journal of Engineering Education
Carfax. Published quarterly.
Manuscripts to: T Becher, University of Sussex.

European Journal of Special Needs
Routledge. Published three times a year.
Manuscripts to: S Hegarty, National Foundation for Educational Research.

European Journal of Teacher Education
Carfax. Published three times a year.
Manuscripts to: M Todeschini, Istituto di Pedagogia, Universita degli
studii, Milan.

Forum for Promoting 3–19 Comprehensive Education
Triangle. Published three times a year.
Manuscripts to: N Whitbread, Beaumont Cottage, East Langton, Market
Harborough.

Gender and Education
Carfax. Published three times a year.
Manuscripts to: C Hughes, Department of Continuing Education, University of Warwick.

International Journal of Disability and Development in Education
University of Queensland Press. Published three times a year.
Manuscripts to: F and E Schonell, Special Education Centre, St Lucia, Australia.

International Journal of Education Research
Pergamon Press. Published 12 times a year.
Manuscripts to: HJ Walberg, University of Illinois, Chicago, USA.

International Journal of Science Education
Taylor and Francis. Published six times a year.
Manuscripts to: JK Gilbert, University of Reading.

International Journal of Technology and Design Education
Kluwer. Published three times a year.
Manuscripts to: The Editor, Kluwer, Dordrecht, The Netherlands.

International Research in Geographical and Environmental Education
La Trobe University Press. Published twice a year.
Manuscripts to: J Lidstone, Queensland University of Technology, Australia.

International Studies in Sociology of Education
Triangle. Published twice a year.
Manuscripts to: L Barton, Division of Education, University of Sheffield.

Journal for Educational Policy
Taylor and Francis. Published six times a year.
Manuscripts to: S Ball, Kings College London.

Journal of Access Studies
Jessica Kingsley. Published twice a year.
Manuscripts to: P Jones, Higher Education Quality Council.

Journal of Aesthetic Education
University of Illinois Press. Published quarterly.
Manuscripts to: RA Smith, Department of Educational Policy Studies, University of Illinois at Urbana-Champaign, Illinois, USA.

Journal of Art and Design Education
Blackwell. Published three times a year.
Manuscripts to: J Swift, University of Central England, Birmingham.

Journal of Biological Education
Institute of Biology. Published quarterly.
Manuscripts to: The Editor, 20–22 Queensberry Place, London.

Journal of Computer Assisted Learning
    Blackwell. Published quarterly.
    Manuscripts to: R Lewis, University of Lancaster.

Journal of Educational Television
    Carfax. Published three times a year.
    Manuscripts to: M Messenger Davies, The London Institute.

Journal of Geography in Higher Education
    Carfax. Published three times a year.
    Manuscripts to: M Healey, Cheltenham and Gloucester College of Higher Education.

Journal of Moral Education
    Carfax. Published three times a year.
    Manuscripts to: MJ Taylor, National Foundation for Educational Research.

Journal of Open and Distance Learning
    Open University/Pitman. Published three times a year.
    Manuscripts to: J Matthews, Regional Academic Services, The Open University.

Journal of Philosophy of Education
    Redwood Books. Published three times a year.
    Manuscripts to: R Smith, University of Durham.

Journal of Teacher Development
    Pitman. Published quarterly.
    Manuscripts to: M Golby, School of Education, University of Exeter.

Management in Education
    Pitman. Published quarterly.
    Manuscripts to: The Editor, Putteridge Bury, University of Luton.

Medical Teacher
    Carfax. Published quarterly.
    Manuscripts to: RM Harden, Ninewells Hospital and Medical School.

Mentoring and Tutoring for Partnership in Learning
    Trentham Books. Published three times a year.
    Manuscripts to: J Egglestone, c/o Trentham Books.

Multicultural Teaching to Combat Racism in School and Community
    Trentham Books. Published three times a year.
    Manuscripts to: G Klein, Department of Education, University of Warwick.

Pastoral Care in Education
    Blackwell. Published six times a year.
    Manuscripts to: R Best, Froebel Institute College, London.

Physics Education
> Institute of Physics. Published three times a year.
> Manuscripts to: Institute of Physics, Bristol.

Quality Assurance in Education
> MCB University Press. Published three times a year.
> Manuscripts to: G McElwee, School of Management, University of Humberside.

Quality in Higher Education
> Carfax. Published three times a year.
> Manuscripts to: L Harvey, Centre for Research into Quality, University of Central England.

Research in Drama Education
> Carfax. Published quarterly.
> Manuscripts to: J Somers, University of Exeter.

Research into Science and Technological Education
> Carfax. Published twice a year.
> Manuscripts to: CR Brown, University of Hull.

Sport, Education and Society
> Carfax. Published quarterly.
> Manuscripts to: C Hardy, University of Loughborough.

Studies in the Education of Adults
> National Institution of Adult and Continuing Education. Published twice a year.
> Manuscripts to: J Wallis, Department of Educational Studies, University of Nottingham.

Teaching and Teacher Education
> Pergamon Press. Published six times a year.
> Manuscripts to: N Bennett, University of Exeter.

Annotated Reading List

American Psychological Association (1983) *Publication Manual of the American Psychological Association*, 3rd edn, Washington, DC: American Psychological Association.
> A guide to the style for formal research papers required by a number of international journals.

Cave, R and Cave, J (1985) *Writing for Promotion and Profit: A guide to educational publishing*, Newmarket: Ron and Joyce Cave Educational Consultants.
> A short, rather oversimplified manual that concentrates on facts rather

than skills and provides some useful tips on getting published. It may help you to understand the contract, once you receive it.

Berry, R (1986) *How to Write a Research Paper*, Oxford: Pergamon.
   A short book that covers a number of technical aspects, such as preparing a bibliography and dealing with footnotes, that I have not had space to cover in this chapter. Worth reading if you are new to publishing and lack a source of expert advice.

Open University Press (1993) *An Equal Opportunities Guide to Language and Image*, Buckingham: Open University Press.
   Many publishers have guides to inclusive language. If yours does not, it is essential that you are aware of the hidden messages that your use of language may convey. The Open University Press guide is very short (19 pages), simple and user-friendly.

Collected Original Sources in Education. Carfax.
   A microfiche journal dealing with original international educational research in full.

The following journals, all published by Carfax, provide summaries of many hundred journal articles and/or books published across the world each year. They are a useful means of identifying the most up-to-date research and debate in particular areas of enquiry within education:

Content Pages in Education
Educational Technology
Higher Education Abstracts
Multicultural Education Abstracts
Research into Higher Education Abstracts
Sociology of Education Abstracts
Special Educational Needs Abstracts
Technical Education and Training Abstracts.

ACKNOWLEDGEMENTS
I am particularly grateful to John Owens of David Fulton Publishers for much of the background information about the publisher's perspective included in this chapter.

   I would like to thank Peter Knight of SEDA, Naomi Roth of Cassell Publishers, Oxford University Press, John Skelton of Open University Press, Liz Cartell of Framework Press, Elisabeth Tribe of Hodder and Stoughton Educational, Pat Lomax of Kogan Page, Jessica Kingsley and John Owens of David Fulton Publishers for their willingness to give up their time to provide me with the information to make this section as useful to the reader as possible.

Appendix: The Use of IT for Analysis in Qualitative Research

Qualitative research involves the analysis of qualitative data, which has come to mean all data that cannot be expressed in numbers. For our purposes this essentially means analysis using any of the following as data: words derived from interviews, narratives, notes of descriptions of events, questionnaires, publications, etc. The initial applications of IT used to help to make sense of such masses of information were database programs.

Setting up a Database

To illustrate the approach, let us consider how to set up a database to record simple personal information on a group of people who have been interviewed. You first must decide what information you want to keep details of – name, address, age, etc. The totality of information on a given person would be known in the jargon as that person's 'record'.

Within the record, information would be organized under a certain number of prespecified headings known as 'fields', which allow you to decide on the precise form in which you are going to record the information. For instance you might decide on fields for personal information such as first name, surname, address, post code, age, sex, etc. The actual information in a given field (eg, the surname Higgins) would be known as the 'entry' in that field.

For some fields you must decide in advance on a standard format or coding for the information, to ensure that all records have the information recorded in the same way. For example, you could decide that entries in the 'sex' field must be the words 'male' or 'female', or you could decide to use the codes 'M' or 'F'. Whatever you decide, you must not use a mix of approaches.

Interrogating the Database

Once all the information has been entered for each of the people, the database can be used to carry out certain operations with the data. Commonly three types of operation can be carried out to varying degrees of complexity depending on the particular program you are using.

The first operation is that of *sorting* the records in some way. It may be that you require the surnames to be in alphabetical order, or the ages to be in ascending order. What you have to do is to nominate first the field (eg, 'surname') and then an organizing criterion for the entries in that field by which you want the records to be sorted (eg, alphabetic order from a to z). For this example, after the sorting is carried out, the whole record for the individual whose entry in the 'surname' field comes first alphabetically, will be treated as the first record in the sorted information, and so on. The sorting operation deals with all the records and just rearranges how they are organized for you the user.

The next operation is that of *searching*. This is used when you wish to consider just a subset of the whole collection of records at your disposal. For example, you might wish to work with just the male interviewees' records. The mechanism is to specify a field and a condition which the entry in the field must satisfy. For our example, you would choose the field 'sex' and specify that the entry must be the word 'male'. This is why you had to have decided on a standard format or coding for certain fields such as this, so that you could be sure of what words to search for.

Another possible search would be for all interviewees who had reached their twenty-first birthday. In general, to carry out such a search you would need to have set up a field in the first place that contained an entry for age in whole numbers of years. Then you could search for the entry in this 'age' field to be a number greater than or equal to '21'. A more complex program might allow you to calculate such information about age from entries containing the interviewee's date of birth.

In general then, a search takes the form of 'field to be searched', 'condition to be satisfied', 'value or attribute to be checked'. More complex searches can be carried out by constructing a combination of simple searches linked together using such words as 'and', 'or' and 'not' (the so-called Boolean operators, named after George Boole the nineteenth century mathematician). To continue with our previous examples, interviewees who were both men and over the age of 21 would be found by conducting a search with the combined conditions of the word 'male' in the 'sex' field and a number greater than or equal to '21' in the field for 'age'. In semi-mathematical form with brackets used to denote each simple search the combined search would have the form:

('sex' the same as 'male') AND ('age' greater than or equal to '21').

At the next level of complexity you might wish to select some interviewees under one set of criteria but also some others under a different set. For instance, say for some reason you wished to consider only those interviewees of pensionable age, then you would need to select men older than 65 but also women older than 60. This search would be built up as follows. First you require for the men the condition:

('sex' the same as 'male') AND ('age' greater than or equal to '65').

Then for the women you need the condition:

('sex' the same as 'female') AND ('age' greater than or equal to '60').

These two conditions are then combined using the Boolean operator OR as follows:

[('sex' the same as 'male') AND ('age' greater than or equal to '65')]
OR
[('sex' the same as 'female') AND ('age' greater than or equal to '60')]

where the square brackets allow you to see the hierarchy under which the conditions will be combined.

The final operation is that of *presentation*, by which we mean taking the results of a sort or search and printing them out on paper or displaying them on the screen in a number of different formats. In its simplest form this might be just printing the full text of a given interviewee's record. It might be printing out the full addresses of all the interviewees in alphabetical order. Some programs will allow presentation of results in various graphical forms, so you could produce histograms, pie charts, scatter diagrams, etc. Some allow statistical calculations to be carried out on the data, so you can calculate and present means, standard deviations, etc.

Having looked at the basic operations of a database, we can now consider how they might be used for our purposes. One example might be when analysing the replies to a questionnaire. A record could be constructed for each respondent, consisting of some fields of personal information about the respondent, including perhaps an identifying number for purposes of later anonymity, together with some fields containing the replies to the questions. Extra fields could then be added, in which you would enter key words from a predetermined list you had decided to use, thus coding certain replies in order to help to categorize them. After all the records had been constructed, they could be searched for replies with similar key words as an initial attempt at analysis.

Types of Qualitative Analysis

In a comprehensive survey, Tesch (1990) identifies 26 distinct qualitative research approaches with varying analysis requirements. Thankfully, for the purposes of our discussion these approaches can be grouped together and, to use her terminology, categorized as being either 'structural' or 'interpretational' analysis. In structural analysis, the data are assumed to have an underlying structure and the researcher's job is to discover it. This would include such approaches as discourse analysis and event structure analysis. In interpretational analysis the researcher organizes the data into categories in an attempt to understand them and hence either analyse them or build a theory about them. This would include such approaches as grounded theory construction, ethnomethodology and symbolic interactionism. For full details see Tesch (1990, pp.94–9).

The structural analysis approach lends itself to the use of databases as already described, albeit now more sophisticated versions with enhanced input, sorting, searching and presentation operations. A second category of programs that can be used for structural analysis are those that work with individual words as data. These are suitable for researchers interested in the uses of language. They work on pieces of text and analyse the structure by producing: *word lists* showing which words occur in the text; *word counts* giving the frequency of occurrence of specified words; *indices* indicating where certain words occur in the text by, for example, line numbering; and *concordances* giving the context in which words appear by presenting the words around them.

The interpretational approach has different requirements. Here the mass of data needs to be broken down into smaller more manageable units, each containing some meaning but preserving the information about its relationship to the whole. These units are then categorized or coded according to some organizing system which the researcher develops from the data. The purpose of categorizing the data is to collect together those units which refer to a particular topic so that each category can be studied first individually and then in relation to the whole. In the process of carrying out this coding for all your data, you usually find that the original categories thought of need some adaptation because of anomalies that you discover as you go along, and so new categories emerge.

For example, one of the authors has surveyed groups of education students about their use of IT with the classes they were working with during periods of school experience. As well as collecting data on frequency and type of use, the students were asked to identify what had assisted or hindered their use of IT in the classroom. The replies were obviously in an open response format and unstructured as it could not be known what the responses were going to be in advance. Thus the interpretational approach had to be taken to allow analysis.

Manual Procedures for Qualitative Analysis

There are many different approaches for carrying out these procedures manually. Some are described in Bogdan and Biklen (1982). They all require that you identify units of the text and then categorize them. Here are a few examples (see also Chapter 3) to give a flavour of what is required:

- You could make multiple photocopies of the data, highlight the units of text in different colours, and then file them under different categories (with some units in more than one file). This approach keeps each unit in its original context on the page, but breaks up the overall flow of the text.
- You could physically cut up the data into units of text (annotated with where they came from, enabling you to reconstruct the context when required), stick them onto index cards and file them by category, or stick units from the same category on one sheet of paper. Again this breaks up the overall structure of the original text.
- You could number each line of the data document, record the beginning and end numbers for each unit, then list the reference numbers for a particular category on an index card. This preserves the form of the original but the categories are difficult to work with, being just lists of line numbers, and you have to return to the originals for the text.
- You could copy or stick the units onto specially prepared cards which have holes round the edge that can be punched out. Each hole position is then designated for a different category and holes are punched out for the categories the unit comes into. The cards can then be searched by inserting a knitting needle through the

holes for a given category, and this selects the subset of cards in that category. The benefit of this approach is that you have a unique card for each text unit which is classifiable with all the categories that unit falls into, and so you have a feel for the totality of categories satisfied by a particular unit. The drawback is that you must have a clear idea beforehand of the categories you are going to use, and it is very difficult to accommodate emerging categories as discussed above.

IT Approach to Qualitative Analysis

All of the manual approaches can become chaotic if you are dealing with large amounts of data, and IT programs are now becoming available that will allow you to carry out on the text all the procedures you require in a purely electronic form. Essentially you are able to mark the beginning and end of the units in the text, attach category codes to each unit, and then carry out searches on these codes, much as we have described for databases. You can search for certain codes and assemble the units of text carrying them; you can carry out Boolean searches on the codes; you can search for occurrences of sequences of codes in the original; you can have a frequency count of the codes prepared; you can recode as new categories emerge. In effect, you can do all that you can do manually and more, without the problems of large quantities of paper and without the degradation of the records that inevitably occurs if you use paper records.

There are many benefits to the IT approach to qualitative analysis:

- It incorporates the best features of the manual approaches, as you do not need multiple copies of the text units to be made, you maintain each unit in its original context, and you can exhibit the totality of classifications that you have decided a given unit should have.
- You can carry out complex searches and sorts more quickly than by hand, which means that you can speculate more widely about possible interpretations of the data and the links that can be made.
- You can handle large quantities of data more easily than in the physical formats, which can quickly become unwieldy and untidy.
- It is easy to add new data, so a small-scale cumulative approach to an investigation can equally easily be adopted.
- You can present your findings in a large variety of different formats and again, as the actual process of presentation takes very

little time, you can experiment with ways of presenting your findings to find the most effective.

One possible disadvantage to the IT approach is one that is common to all IT uses and that is the amount of time it takes to become familiar with a particular package. However, the manual processes of data analysis are themselves time-consuming and it may well be that once you have become a confident user of the facilities on offer, you save time both at the initial stage of categorization and coding of the data as well as in the analysis of it.

References

Bogdan, R and Biklen, S (1982) *Qualitative Research for Education: An introduction to theory and methods*, Boston, MA: Allyn and Bacon.

Tesch, R (1990) *Qualitative Research: Analysis types and software tools*, London: Falmer Press.

Index